DAMAGE DONE

DAMAGE DONE

A MOUNTIE'S MEMOIR
From Hurt to Hopeful, from Horses to Healing

DEANNA LENNOX

HarperCollins*Publishers*Ltd

Damage Done
Copyright © 2015 by Deanna Lennox

Published by HarperCollins Publishers Ltd

First edition

HarperCollins books may be purchased for educational, business or sales promotional use through our Special Markets Department.

HarperCollins Publishers Ltd
2 Bloor Street East, 20th Floor
Toronto, Ontario, Canada
M4W 1A8

www.harpercollins.ca

Library and Archives Canada Cataloguing in Publication information is available upon request

ISBN 978-1-44342-461-5

Printed and bound in the United States
RRD 9 8 7 6 5 4 3 2 1

For my family—Jerry, Skylar and Kassidy

CONTENTS

O ut of the corner of my eye, I catch movement. It's mid-afternoon, so I use one hand to shield the blazing sun and look up to see a hawk off in the distance circling high in the sky. I am walking in the grass, taking deep breaths and smelling the open air. I am in the middle of a 30-hectare field with thick trees on one side and a large grassy area on the other. Working as a police officer, I have learned the importance of being aware of my surroundings. I complete a visual sweep of my immediate area, and I notice a few obstacles that could be used for cover, if it comes to that.

I know Maggie is here somewhere and odds are she already knows I'm here looking for her. We've been through this scenario before. She knows her options are limited and that all the exits are blocked, but still she runs even though there's nowhere to go—why does she always have to run?

I know she's not going to just give up and let herself be caught. Maggie has a strong sense of survival, and I suppose I should be glad that her first instinct is to run instead of fight—although I know she has fight in her too. I take cover behind a piece of farm equipment. Even though I may not entirely want to, I have to leave this safe place and expose myself if I'm ever going to get this done. I've chased bad people throughout my career, and yet this field leaves me feeling incredibly unsettled. I urge myself to move forward, staying alert and focused. One wrong move and a five-minute job could turn into an all-day event.

Truth be told, I'm concerned more about her friends than about Maggie herself. They can be unpredictable, and if I don't keep my wits about me, they can come up from behind. They have interfered in the past and have shown little regard for me or any authority I think I might have in this situation.

Maggie is my palomino quarter horse mare. And what I have just described is my first solo attempt to catch her in a field. Horses are living and thinking beings, with their own ideas, likes and dislikes, and even though they are huge animals, they are also prey animals, and their actions are the result of a prey mentality. They are constantly assessing their surroundings, stressed and aware that a lion or other predator could be skulking around in the bushes waiting to pounce. For survival, horses live in herds and they have a hierarchy that is tested and retested daily. The philosophy of the horse is lead, follow or get out of the way.

To have the relationship with my horse that I wanted, I would have to earn Maggie's trust—and respect. Right now she trusted me, she knew I wouldn't hurt her, but she was walking all over me in the respect department. My definition of respect or of how to attain respect is this: you do what you are told or suffer the consequences. What were the appropriate consequences for

Maggie? Beating her wasn't an option for a variety of reasons, not least because any trust would be lost.

I would have to earn my mare's respect by giving her what she needed, and she needed to feel that I was a worthy leader—a force to be reckoned with, but not to be feared.

Horses, as prey animals, have a primal instinct to run from what they fear. As a predator, and as a police officer, my instinct was to control and subdue. Do it or else, was my thinking then. Everything I had never liked about authority, everything I hated, I had become. And Maggie—of course—ran from that.

How, I wondered, had someone so skeptical of authority become so authoritarian? Why had I changed? Where did it start?

CHAPTER ONE

Nowhere to Run

Damage Done: *A Mountie's Memoir* tells my story. I was a young woman who joined the Royal Canadian Mounted Police with the highest of ideals, but sixteen years on the job left me feeling bitter and broken. What helped to heal me was a connection with horses—and this, I hope and trust, is one powerful lesson of the book. Another lesson? That it's possible to heal.

For many years, I was a "first responder," the first on the scene of crimes or accidents or domestic violence. Police officers, firefighters, paramedics, corrections officers, soldiers in war or aiding in national disasters, social workers, nurses: we are all first responders exposed almost daily to occupational stress. We are expected to act calmly and professionally in the face of terrible human suffering and carnage.

As an RCMP officer, you arrive at the scene of a car crash, with people inside dying—and not quietly; it's staggering what tons of cut metal can do to a human body. You go to a house where someone has blown his head off with a shotgun or hung himself. You respond to a call and find the shattered mother of a four-year-old child who has died in his sleep and physically stop this woman from taking her own life. You enter an apartment where a mother is astride and beating her child while the father looks on. After all the times you've notified next of kin who will never see their loved ones again, you ask yourself: how do you console the inconsolable?

It's expected that RCMP officers will put the impact of all this behind them. Get on with the job. No looking back. And some of us do manage—or at least appear to. Here are some staggering facts: Members of the RCMP with thirty-five or more years of service typically collect their pensions for just two years before they die. Divorce rates among some first responders are as high as 84 percent. One in four first responders struggles with alcoholism. The numbers vary widely from study to study, but it's thought that 10 to 30 percent of first responders suffer from post-traumatic stress disorder (PTSD). By a factor of two, they are more likely to die from suicide than in the line of duty. It was reported that twenty-three first responders committed suicide in Canada between April and October 2014, most of them in Ontario. Finally, the life expectancy of first responders is fifteen years less than that of the general population.

What police officers typically do with their job-induced stress and anxiety, their despair and depression, their sleeplessness and nightmares, is bury it all in what I call an internal Dumpster—and we keep on piling stuff in there even when the Dumpster is clearly overflowing. Members of the force soon isolate themselves from society, only keeping the company of other officers. Only they, we say to ourselves, truly understand.

We tell war stories and at times drink heavily, but that often only makes matters worse. Marriages and relationships unravel, health declines and the toll is heavy yet invisible. Think of Mounties and most people think of the Musical Ride and the red tunics. *Damage Done: A Mountie's Memoir* takes you into the contemporary life of an officer in the RCMP, peeling back the glossy images to reveal what's underneath.

Many, many first responders suffer from occupational stress injuries. I did, without a doubt. One evening my husband entered a room where I was "watching TV"—except I wasn't, because the TV was off. I was staring into darkness. And even now, although I have accepted my new "normal," I have moments that serve to remind me that my life is not the same as it used to be.

I tried traditional medicine, alternative medicine, counselling, meditation, yoga and various other methods to deal with my demons—with varying degrees of success. Only by chance did I come to horses. My daughter was desperate to take riding lessons, and this led me to the majestic Riversong Ranch in the eastern foothills of the Canadian Rockies. During one of my first sessions, I was working on the ground (not in the saddle) with a horse called Razzy—a gorgeous black Thoroughbred rescued from the racetrack. He suffers from post-traumatic stress disorder himself after a long history of abuse. We were together in an enclosed circular pen about 15 metres in diameter. I was standing in the middle of the pen and Razzy began to race around the enclosure. The more I tried to control him—not with a lead rope but with my body language, as I had been taught—the faster he went. I could hear the clang when his body bounced off the steel bars of the pen as he tried to find his way out. Out and away from me.

Razzy, I would learn, was reacting to nothing other than the high-intensity energy I had brought into the pen. Kathryn Kincannon-Irwin, an owner of the ranch, told me that I had better start breathing and calming myself down. My response: I thought I *was* calm! I tried to soften my shoulders and move slowly, but the horse wasn't reading just my outside; he was reading my inside. When I finally understood how to deflate myself by breathing deeply and calming my mind, Razzy began to slow down. Finally he softened to a point where he followed me around the pen like a puppy. It was my first lesson in being responsible for the energy I bring to every situation. It was also my first lesson in the power of breath.

Out of that and other experiences with horses came the idea for what I would eventually call the annual War Horse Symposium, whereby people from a variety of organizations could come together to share information and work with horses. I have held five of these symposiums, starting in 2010. The one in the fall of 2012 was attended by the Honourable Colonel (Retired) Donald Ethell, the Lieutenant-Governor of Alberta.

The results have been extraordinary and gratifying, not least because these symposiums—and this book, perhaps—will raise the profile of the thousands of frontline service providers who struggle with occupational stress.

———

When I began my career in the Royal Canadian Mounted Police, friends and family told me that I should write my experiences down. One day, they said, I could write a book. The furthest thing from my mind was to write a book. Ever.

I would describe myself as an extremely private person—those who know me would say that is an understatement. There was a time when I could not have contemplated putting parts of myself on display. But here I am.

I have come to realize that something needs to be said. I have secrets I need to share. My goal is to give insight into a profession and lifestyle that most people are only able to live vicariously through television, movies and novels. *Damage Done* describes the rise and fall of one Mountie, but it doesn't end there. Revealing my innermost secrets is an effort on my part to cast out ghosts that continue to haunt me—even though I'm no longer working as a police officer on the street. My theory is that purging myself of these events will allow them to live on somewhere off in the distance, instead of so close to home. And by bringing my own experiences out in the open, I hope to start a conversation.

One secret is that the life of a Mountie is not as glorious as one might think. I am in the process of accepting that my experiences are a part of me, that they helped make me who I am today, and yet at times I am unable to move forward because my mind continues to take me back to places where my heart no longer wants to be. Police officers and other first responders are a carefully selected—and self-selected—group of individuals who come to this work with a certain degree of innocence. We are forged in battle and we enter the fray. Both our organizations and the public expect, and first responders themselves expect, that we will simply take what comes our way in stride.

The truth is that I was not prepared to see the things I saw or do the things I did as a police officer on the street. I was not equipped with the superpowers required to attend a crime scene where children had violently perished or to watch people take their own lives right before my eyes—and, in the name of professionalism, not shed a tear. I was not equipped to move on to the next call, or when off duty to somehow still function as a "normal" person in society.

The majority of first responders do not start their mornings wanting to be labelled a hero; their main intention is to survive the day and go home to their families. At one point in the late 2000s, an internal RCMP report estimated that some 60 to 70 percent of RCMP members who are off duty on medical leave are dealing with psychologically related issues such as post-traumatic stress disorder and depression. The lack of research and statistics make it difficult to track today. Shining a light on this part of our job is not about gaining sympathy, but it is about empathy. The reality is that we typically come into this profession physically and mentally healthy, and we far too often leave it feeling tired, bitter and damaged. We often feel pushed out the door as it slams behind us, only to be replaced by a newer and most times younger version, and thus the cycle begins again. We are left to pick up the psychological pieces that just don't seem to fit back together no matter what we do.

In my journey to put my pieces back together, I began to understand that police officers are not the only group facing this crisis. Everyone will nod in agreement when it is proposed that the military deserves specialized training to help heal the psychologically wounded. But I've been involved in more than one conversation in which a psychologist or police officer has suggested that the police are actually worse off than the military. Members of the military generally are deployed once for a relatively short period of time, whereas police officers deal with trauma day after day. The counter-argument is made that soldiers are exposed to intense violence and human suffering. They put their lives on the line to protect our freedom and our way of life. The two groups actually argue about which group is the most psychologically wounded! We have created a hierarchy of trauma in an effort to decide who is most deserving of the resources. We are forced to compare ourselves and pick sides when we are already on the same side. We all deserve the opportunity and the resources to live healthy and balanced lives. If soldiers get specialized treatment, so should police officers and, indeed, all people who have chosen to serve our country and our communities. My point is this: we *all* deserve to be healthy and feel good—and I can't say that I always felt that way.

In my early days as a police officer, I believed that the military and police were the only professions exposed to real trauma. I never considered the firefighter who tries for hours to resuscitate a toddler only to have that child die in his arms. I never considered the social worker who deals with abused children who live in dysfunctional family situations. I was in "the bubble," and in the bubble, it's always worse inside than it is outside. But once I really listened to the stories of those "out there," I realized that though their experiences might be different, the impact on them was just as serious. Trauma manifests itself in the same way in all of us. The social worker can drink herself to sleep with the same brand of vodka as a police officer. The connection is that we're all struggling to understand our humanity.

An ex-volunteer firefighter shared his story with me, and it opened my eyes. Jeremy came from a long line of volunteer firefighters. He and his brother were competitive with each other and so when his older brother became a volunteer, he knew he had to follow. He became a volunteer at age fourteen. Other volunteers tried to shield him from fatal motor vehicle accidents, but his desire to partake in all aspects of the job wore them down. By age sixteen, he was the captain of the team and, he told me, "doing things many adults have never done."

He eventually went on to be a fire chief in a rural community, and that's where everything began to unravel. He attended a motor vehicle collision where both vehicles had burst into flames, killing all occupants. Involved in the accident was a family member of someone he worked with, a friend, and he recognized the person as he was dealing with the incident. "I did my job," he wrote in the War Horse Awareness Foundation newsletter, "but something was different."

A year later he attended another collision—this one close to the location of the previous accident—in which the vehicle involved was smoking and the risk was high of another fireball. He arrived at the scene and was putting on his protective gear, preparing himself for the task at hand, when suddenly he froze. He recalls the witnesses and the driver of one of the vehicles screaming and crying. He remembers the RCMP on the scene asking him questions, but it was as though they were speaking a different language. He walked away, and when the fire crew arrived, he got into his vehicle and left. After remaining at his desk for most of the day, he decided to write his resignation letter. He wondered how he could lead when he couldn't do the job himself anymore. He elected at that point to seek professional help, but in his mind "he was done, a has-been."

Jeremy was convinced that he was no longer of value to the people he had vowed to help and protect. He felt that the job had broken him. But he also came to a realization: "that to lead by example may not mean you have to be standing tall, tough and proud at every incident." Leading your team means ensuring that the help they need to do their jobs is accessible and that they know being affected is acceptable and normal. "Our job is to help people," he wrote, "but we need to realize that sometimes we ourselves need help."

What the story illustrates for me is my blind spot. I was a first responder too preoccupied with my own job to have any understanding of what other first responders had to deal with. A volunteer firefighter was low on my list of people needing help for on-the-job trauma. Jeremy went into the job at a young age looking for fun and excitement; he could not have foreseen the price to be paid.

Hearing his story made me understand more than ever that while the roles of first responders may vary, we are all in this together—which is why I created a non-profit organization called the War Horse Awareness Foundation.

Trauma manifests itself in similar ways in everyone—post-traumatic stress disorder (PTSD), depression, addictions, sleep disorders. I was diagnosed with major depression with symptoms of post-traumatic stress disorder several years ago—and assigned a few other labels as well.

While learning to deal with the traumatic experiences I faced on the street and within my own organization, I discovered the healing nature of horses. Through my work with them, I have not overcome my depression, but I have learned to understand it. I no longer suffer from depression or PTSD; I have learned to *live* with depression and PTSD. When I ceased to be who I was, I finally found who I am.

CHAPTER TWO

Baby Blue Epaulettes

I'm sure I raised a few eyebrows when I accepted the offer to go through the training process with Canada's most recognized police force. I was generally a good-hearted person who never got into a whole lot of trouble—despite my reputation for having a bit of an attitude. My biggest challenge: authority.

But I was also undisciplined and self-centred and had led a pretty sheltered life up to that point. Joining the RCMP ultimately would force me to grow up hard and quick. I would like to say that I rebelled only against authority that was improperly exercised, but the truth is that I had a knack for pushing people's buttons, and I used it often. People tend to show their true selves when they are stressed or angry, and I was interested in seeing how people really are. I've always believed it's important to pay attention to the first time someone shows you his or her true colours, because it won't be long before you see those colours again.

I particularly took issue with bullies. Not because I was ever bullied extensively, but because I always had a soft spot for those who never got to reveal themselves because somebody else wouldn't let them. Authority based on a foundation of fear is equal to bullying, and I would fight it every step of the way. I don't remember a time that I have been intimidated by anyone in authority. This ended up serving me well during my career in dealing with individuals involved in organized crime, or really anyone who felt they were in a position of power, albeit in their own little world.

Showing respect for people in authority is completely different from giving all your own personal power away, which is what fear-based authority expects. Initially I can, and will, respect your position, but treat me like an individual who has her own thoughts and feelings. I'm sure I could devote an entire chapter to the subject of the wise use of authority, and compassionate leadership, but the purpose of bringing it up here is to offer a point of origin. And I find it hard to believe how terribly wrong it all went, how far off my own beliefs I eventually drifted.

In my youth I was not frightened of authority, as some were. I believed that those in positions of power should have flexibility and understanding. But maybe, I came to think, that ideal was unattainable. I was kicked off high school basketball teams and soccer teams because I didn't like being disciplined as a group for the infractions of one or two individuals. In retrospect, I guess I just didn't like being disciplined, period. I always reacted to words or actions that were, in my view, unjust.

In college I enrolled in a criminal justice program. Mr. Rudolph was an instructor in college who dealt out "interesting punishment." He asked during a class what the purpose was of the police, and I answered, "To serve and protect." It was a smart-ass answer that was met with an unexpected and creative consequence: he made me write out Section 394 of the Criminal Code—on the powers of arrest. It wasn't that long a section, maybe half a page. The trick? Each word had to be written in a different colour. He was actually my favourite instructor, and I went back to visit him often.

I was always athletic in my youth, and I wanted to be a part of making the world a better place, so becoming a police officer seemed like a perfect fit. Sign me up, I as much as said. And they did. I was twenty-three years old.

I went through the screening process quickly and was given a date to start training at the Royal Canadian Mounted Police training facility, also known as Depot Division, in Regina, Saskatchewan.

In February 1996, I drove there from my home in southern Alberta. The roads were in good condition considering it was winter, and there was an average amount of snow on the ground for that time of year. Though I had lived in Saskatchewan briefly when I was younger, this was the first time I had ever been in the province's capital.

I turned off the Trans-Canada Highway and followed the signs for Depot. I was ready for the drive to be over, but I was also feeling a bit nervous about this new adventure. I was about to get six-and-a-half-months' training for a lifetime of police work.

It wasn't long before I saw the large white sign with that familiar RCMP logo—the buffalo, crown and laurel of maple leaves, and the words in gold on blue, *Maintiens le droit*. (It means "Defend the law," or according to some translations, "Uphold the right.")

I had arrived.

I felt a flutter in the pit of my stomach as I approached the manned booth at the front gates. I explained who I was and the guard directed me to the main building. The man sitting at the desk there asked me for identification, and as I dug out my wallet, I said, "I'm here to start training. I'm with Troop 25." He handed me a map and told me where to park my vehicle. He then put a star next to a building on the map and roughly pointed in the direction I needed to drive to unload my belongings.

Since 1885, the RCMP has trained its members at this facility, which is similar to a military base. Mostly made of brick, the structures appeared old but were in good condition despite the number of recruits they had seen through the years. If only those buildings could talk, I was sure they would have stories to tell. The buildings featured regularly spaced windows and reminded me of an older elementary school I once attended. I could sense the tradition in the air, and, for the first time, I could feel the gravity of what I had signed up to do. I was embarking on a journey to become part of the greatest police force in the world. If I could make it through this training, I would be a Canadian Mountie.

I opened the door to get out of my vehicle and immediately felt that cold, crisp Saskatchewan air on my face. After grabbing my suitcase, I walked across the road to my dorm. As I climbed up the outside stairs, I wondered what exactly waited for me behind those doors at the top. I realized I had reached a point of no return. I didn't know anyone who would be in my troop with me. I didn't know what the dorm would be like or how many other women would be there. I felt alone and isolated, even though I was minutes away from the second largest city in the province.

But for the cold, I probably would have stood at the threshold of the second floor for a few moments longer, but the chill wind running down the back of my neck pushed me forward. I opened the door and my nostrils were immediately offended by strong scents that I would later identify as shoe polish and gun-cleaning oil. I entered and passed by one room where several people were sitting on chairs with boots in one hand and cloths stained with shoe polish in the other. I heard hair dryers going and wondered briefly why some individuals were lighting the tips of their boots with lighters. I passed through another door into a large, cavernous room where there were more beds and what struck me as an abnormally high number of ironing boards. I was greeted by a group of young women residing at this end of the dorm.

One of them enthusiastically announced, "We're from Troop 16 and we're your big brother and big sister troop." It turned out that every troop is assigned a big brother troop, which is a group of trainees halfway through the program. They take on the responsibility of helping a new troop become adjusted to the environment and answering any questions.

When I think back to that moment, I realize that I had no idea what was in store for me.

I started training in the month of February, that most cruel of the cold winter months on the prairie. Troop 25 comprised twenty-four people from different walks of life and from all over the country. There were two males in our troop over the age of forty, one female who was just twenty-one years old. The men were housed in one dorm and the women in another, each with multiple floors. There were thirty-two beds in one dorm, shared sinks in the bathroom, and—my personal non-favourite—a common shower.

In the dorm, a long walkway ran down the middle separating one side of the room from the other. Sixteen beds on the right, sixteen beds on the left. Two beds shared a space called a "pit"— an open area for our own dressers and closets. I shared a pit with one person, and my bed was pushed against another bed, separated only by a snore board. The person on the other side of my snore board shared a pit area with the next person down the line, and so on. My pit was located second from the end, which was nice in a way, because being close to the door made me feel a little less claustrophobic.

Unfortunately, I was on the side of the dorm farthest from the bathroom. So every single morning, sporting my bed-head and wearing my pyjamas, I had to pack all my toiletries and walk the gauntlet. I was young and living intimately with *thirty-one* strangers (the nine in my troop plus a few bodies from other troops). The area was completely open, with no doors and no privacy. And who would have thought that women actually snore! This represented one of the biggest challenges I had faced to that point in my life. Even in college, aside from one excruciating year, I had always lived alone. Sharing one big living area with dozens of other people effectively wrenched me out of my comfort zone.

I really have no idea how some of the older and more mature recruits were able to maintain their sanity. Living with all these other people was far and away the hardest part of the almost-seven-month training period. Every other weekend I would drive to my parents' place in southern Alberta to get a break from my claustrophobic digs. Some recruits from Ontario with spouses and children back home never saw them during all that time. I wondered, How did they stand it?

The atmosphere at Depot was a blend of competitiveness and camaraderie. In physical or firearms classes, for example, we were keeping score. We supported each other, but at the same time, each of us wanted to be at or near the top. It became clear as time passed, though, that not all of us were going to make it through training, and as that reality set in, tensions rose. It never, ever occurred to me that I would not graduate. But in the end, three of my troop of twenty-four dropped out. Injury, illness and circumstance all took their toll.

In one case, a female cadet withdrew—and that was a source of relief because it was clear to us all that she was a weak link. But in another case, an older male cadet left after suffering an injury, and that was a blow to morale. This man was seen as a father figure, someone with wisdom and life experience, who never allowed himself to get caught up in the drama at Depot, as some did.

For the first two weeks of training we walked around in civilian clothes—dress pants and a dress shirt. After two weeks we were required to wear our grey RCMP uniform shirts with chocolate brown pants and running shoes. Everyone's shirt had striped epaulettes on the shoulder to indicate how long we'd been in training. New recruits like me started training with blue epaulettes and no stripes. As we progressed through training, at set times our epaulettes were exchanged for ones with stripes—

from one up to three. The graduating troop was distinguishable by their three black stripes and one red stripe. Once we became sworn police officers, the baby blue epaulettes would be removed—gone forever.

We had not yet learned how to march, so we had to run (more like a shuffle), in time and all together, everywhere we went. As we progressed through our training, we "earned" the right to wear our "blues"—RCMP-issue pants with the yellow stripe down the side. Once in our issued pants, we were expected to march to different classes and buildings on campus. The highest milestone of deportment was breaches and high brown boots.

High brown boots were worn with the prestigious red serge, and it took hours upon hours of boot shining to make them look as impressive as they did. Traditions and tips on how to shine them—involving everything from cigarette lighters to hair dryers—were passed from troop to troop. But at the end of the day, how much time we put into it was what mattered most. I had never pegged myself as a boot shiner, but once you see how good it looks, spit and polish becomes almost an obsession. I may not like the illusion of the red serge, but the most recognizable uniform in the whole world enjoys that standing with good reason. When put together with pride, the uniform is impressive.

———

Going to Depot was like going to college. The difference: my classmates never varied. I was part of this group of twenty-four, and for nearly seven months, we spent almost every day together. Our troop was assigned three facilitators, who were responsible for teaching us about the law and other applicable academic skills that would be required during our career. They were also responsible for getting us through the training. Currently, the RCMP cadet training program is broken down into 785 hours, with assigned instructors for all classes: applied police sciences (at 373 hours, the largest single allotment), firearms training, self-defence, physical education, driving and, of course, drill and deportment.

The physical education instructors and the drill instructors were, for the most part, responsible for administering appropriate discipline. There were consequences for individuals showing up to class late or not being prepared, and, because Depot was a "team sport," the entire troop suffered those consequences. Every troop at some time during its training was subjected to an "AA," also known as an "Attitude Adjustment." This usually involved running until you puked or doing push-ups until your arms and chest burned beyond feeling. AA was meant to push people to the brink, and it did.

Like those you see on television and in the movies, drill instructors at RCMP Depot yelled at the top of their lungs about two inches from your face. They were not only teaching new recruits how to march but also were responsible for teaching us the standards for dress and deportment. Dress—which I considered to be the least important part of the whole training experience— was actually considered the most important in training.

When a troop was punished, it would be "busted down" (back to brown pants and running shoes) and would have to earn back its uniform blues and boots. I soon came to understand that in the RCMP, image is everything. I struggled with that ideology then and I still do. Being competent or a hard worker didn't matter if you didn't look like you knew what you were doing. The reliance on the illusion of the mighty red serge is an issue that plagues an organization that has so much more to offer.

Some people took the whole drill experience pretty seriously. Our main instructor took herself seriously too. She never even cracked a smile. As the training progressed, most instructors tended to enhance a sense of camaraderie by softening, but our drill instructor never did. In one drill class we had a replacement instructor—the most notorious drill instructor in the RCMP. For years he had screamed and struck fear into the hearts of more than his share of recruits. We were practising our marching in the drill hall one day, and he yelled at me from across the room for not raising my arms high enough. Here was a challenge I couldn't resist! It was game on.

I waited for a few minutes and dropped my arms ever so slightly. I knew he would catch it, and he did. He called the troop to a halt and made a beeline for me, stick in hand. He stopped right in front of me, took a deep breath and leaned into my space. As he was about to let his saliva fly, I leaned back and smiled a little. He paused and then started to laugh. We made brief eye contact, and from that day on, he and I had a new understanding. I wasn't buying into the whole fear game, which wasn't any fun at all for him, so he moved on to someone else. We both knew that although he had made a living at playing a bully, in the end he was just a man who, thankfully, didn't take himself as seriously as everyone else did.

The RCMP employs more than 29,000 men and women, arranged in a dizzying assortment of ranks—from one commissioner at the top to almost 12,000 constables at the bottom. Of all the police forces in Canada, the RCMP is the most paramilitary. The last time I looked there were 9 deputy commissioners, 25 assistant commissioners, 51 chief superintendents, 186 superintendents, 440 inspectors, 16 staff sergeants major, 942 staff sergeants, more than 2,000 sergeants and almost 4,000 corporals.

The paramilitary feel of the force may explain why Depot put such an emphasis on marching. Every day started the same way, with morning parade. Morning parade was essentially a role call for every troop in training. Cadets would scramble out of the dorm doors at 6 a.m. to meet up with their troop. The drill instructor had previously assessed the troop and placed everyone according to height. The taller cadets were positioned in the back row and the shorter ones in the front. Your place never changed. Each morning we would march to the drill hall in order of our troop number, the most senior troop arriving last.

I was positioned in the middle of the front row. I remember taking my place as our "right marker" waited for everyone to settle before issuing his first command. Every troop had a right marker—the designated leader of a troop. That individual was tasked with extra responsibilities such as ensuring the troops arrive at class on time, deciding what uniform we would wear for the day and making certain when we marched that we did so in time and on the appropriate foot. We were lined up facing him. Our right marker came to attention by lifting his left foot and slamming it down at a 45-degree angle to his right foot. He proceeded to call the rest of us to attention, and in unison we each lifted our left foot and stomped it in place. From top to bottom, we truly were at attention—on alert, waiting to respond to the next instruction. Our eyes forward—not wandering, standing tall, chest pushed out and arms rigidly at our sides with our fists clenched and thumbs pointed down the seams of our trousers. Our thumbs covered the holes formed by our curled fingers. Next came "Eyes right," instructing us all to turn our heads to the right. The next command was "Dress"—the signal for us to shuffle and align our shoulders with the person on our right. Once our right marker was confident we were aligned, he commanded our stare back to the front.

When it was our troop's turn to make the march to the drill hall, we were ordered to start. We began by marching on the spot and were directed by our right marker to break off into groups of eight—four from the front row and four from the back. This is where it got tricky for the right marker. It was his job to call the commands on the proper foot. If he set us into motion on the wrong foot, our timing would be off, and that was not acceptable to the drill instructors.

We marched in time to the drill hall. Our right marker would occasionally yell out which foot we should be on—"*Left . . . left, right, left.*" The drill instructor's pronunciation was "*Eft . . . eft, ight, eft.*" For some reason the first letter wasn't pronounced, and they all had their own unique way of yelling for the troops to come to attention. Even they had a need to exercise their own sense of individuality.

It was an impressive display when everyone was in time. The best part, though, was transitioning into the drill hall from outside. I can still hear the sound of boots hitting pavement, then turning into a thunderous noise on hardwood flooring. There's no other sound like it.

Drill was a thorn in my side for my entire stay at Depot. I never took to the philosophy of breaking people down and building them back up again. We were called to attention by whoever was doing the inspection, and he or she would walk around and look at everyone's uniform and posture.

We were taught to stand, and were expected to stand, a certain way—our feet had to be a particular width apart, toes pointed out at a certain angle, with our shoulders back and arms at our sides. We would then be ordered to a more relaxed position of standing at ease, and then into a stand easy position. Our uniforms were all expected to be impeccable, crisp and ironed and looking exactly the same. I detested morning parade and often forgot either my nametag or some other noticeable part of my uniform. Once I actually forgot to put on my tie. I never was a morning person.

The slightest flaw in one's uniform would be cause for attendance at "Bozo Parade"—yet another inspection before you could go for breakfast. One morning I was standing at attention, already at Bozo Parade, with five or six other cadets from various troops. One of the drill instructors, who was at least a foot taller than me, hovered over me and wrote *B-O-Z-O* in the dust on the brim of my forage cap. He said the letters as he wrote them and he had the biggest smile on his face. I knew what it meant: same time, same place, next morning.

After our morning inspection and roll call, we marched to the Mess for breakfast. We were free to leave the Mess and march back by ourselves to our dorm. If we were scheduled to go to the range or the driving course, we would change into appropriate clothing and meet at a specified time to march to the bus. Most of our time was spent in the Applied Sciences building with our troop facilitators. This was normally a classroom setting with the curriculum broken down into several modules focused on knowledge about law enforcement and problem-solving skills. After time in the classroom, we would gather once again outside in formation and march to the next class.

After our last morning class, we would march over to the Mess Hall again for lunch. Just outside the cafeteria was an area to hang up coats and hats or forage caps. Inside was a regular buffet-style cafeteria with a seating area. If I didn't like what was being served, there was another area that offered bread and sandwich meat. Fussy eater that I am, I ate a lot of bologna while in training.

The afternoon would start off the same as the morning. We would line up and march as a troop to the next class. Unless you were injured or seriously ill, you were required to go to every class with your troop and in formation. There were plenty of rules, and if you didn't follow them, you and your troop would suffer the consequences. If you met an officer along the way, you were required to salute. We were also not allowed to walk or march on the sidewalks, which were reserved for civilians and sworn members.

Our day ended with our last scheduled class and then we would march back to the dorms. There was a brief period of downtime before supper was served in the Mess Hall. After the meal, my focus shifted to polishing boots, ironing my uniforms or cleaning my firearm.

Once those tasks were completed, I would think about the next day. My shined boots were beside my bed and my gym bag was packed with whatever clothing or accessories I needed for classes the next morning. The time before bed was devoted to that. Preparation was the key to surviving training. Socializing was often done during hours of polishing and ironing, but there were also bouts of downtime during which I enjoyed listening to music while lying on my luxury single foam bed. When I stayed for the weekend, I spent time with my troop off the base. I also played soccer on a local women's team. But most often during the week, while others sought comfort in conversation, I sought it in solitude and silence, as I always had.

I had kept a journal since I was a teenager—my attempt at making sense of an often confusing world. An introverted and private person, I wrote in order to process the things that came my way. This was my diary, and for my eyes only.

At Depot, our instructors urged us all to keep a journal, which we kept in a drawer by our beds. But we were not gathering "private thoughts." Our instructors were allowed to read our journals and even insert comments. One day I wrote in my journal that I did not understand why we were doing all this marching.

"You will," wrote my drill instructor in the margin.

And eventually I did understand. Drill was all about image. The Musical Ride performed the same function. If you march (or ride) well and in precision, it creates the impression that you are good at what you do. Drill was about building confidence and pride and discipline—and looking sharp in serge.

Drill was just one aspect of being at Depot that was challenging. We did what we had to do to survive, and if that meant marching here, there and everywhere, that's what we did. I was up early in the morning—much earlier than when I was in college. I had found it difficult to make it to my 8 a.m. English class on a regular basis, so getting up and being ready to go at 6 a.m. was tough. The days were physically and mentally taxing, and our evenings were spent getting ready for the next day. The days were entirely structured, with very little "free time" in between. We were now part of a system, a finely tuned machine. And in order for the machine to run smoothly, there were things we would all have to learn to do quickly and efficiently.

––––

The first week or so at Depot, we were instructed on how to make our beds. The slightest wrinkle anywhere was unacceptable. A wire clothes hanger was the multi-purpose tool we used to smooth wrinkles in the sheets and top blanket, to tuck the corner of the top cover at a 45-degree angle under the mattress and to measure. The turned-over portion of the sheet had to be precisely a hanger's length from the top of the bed, and the fold itself had to be precisely the width of half a hanger.

I found the whole process cumbersome, not to mention confusing, but there was an incentive program. If your bed-making wasn't up to standard, you might be forced to spend hours picking up your entire pit area after a tornado blew through in the form of a drill instructor. Our living areas were inspected regularly, and the last thing anyone wanted to do at the end of a long day was to clean up overturned mattresses, drawers that had been emptied by being turned upside down or piles of clothes ripped out of closets. Privacy for recruits was basically non-existent. Our living area was open to the public during tours, and inspections were carried out day and night.

During my almost two hundred days of training, two in particular stand out as the most unpleasant. The first was the day my troop was scheduled to be mass pepper-sprayed. Every cadet of every troop is required to experience the effects of OC (oleoresin capsicum) pepper spray, and no one is authorized to carry it on duty unless he or she has been exposed. Pepper "spray" is a misnomer: the substance in the canister is like liquid fire in a squirt gun.

Some simple rules applied during this exercise: if you turned your face away (voluntarily or not) or closed your eyes while being sprayed, you would be sprayed again. There was no escape. You *would* experience the full effects of pepper spray. For the instructors, this was a fun day. If you think they felt sorry for us in any way or were content to give just a short blast, you couldn't be more wrong.

Once each cadet received his or her allotted dose of pepper spray, we were required to stay on our feet and take a few steps over to someone holding a dark blue striking pad (a flat target such as trainers hold in the boxing ring), which was supposed to simulate a "bad guy."

The training scenario was this: We were in an altercation with someone, and our pepper spray either had been taken away and used against us, or the bad guy had his own spray. After being sprayed, each of us was to engage the bad guy by grabbing him and giving him three knees to the stomach, and then we were to walk calmly (freaking out because your eyes and face were on fire was not acceptable) to the decontamination area. This was a big tub of water that you could stick your face into, and then your assigned partner would lead you outside to fresh air. The point of the exercise was to make us aware that even if we were injured or placed at significant disadvantage by pepper spray, we were not completely incapacitated. We could maintain our composure, continue the fight and still win. I'm not sure which was worse—eventually getting sprayed, or first watching everyone ahead of me go through the torturous process of being doused with the equivalent of liquid fire.

The wait was long, but finally it was my turn. By this time, I just wanted to get it over with. Our instructor had told us that fair-skinned people usually experience the worst reactions—not good news for many, but a small glimmer of hope for me. Maybe I would be one of the few exceptions who had no reaction at all. Oh, who was I kidding? I walked over to the designated spot, turned around and faced my "executioner"—at least that's what it felt like. I saw the spray shoot out of the canister. It's a challenging task to be asked to combat the involuntary reaction of closing your eyes when something is about to hit them, especially when your mind already knows what pain is coming. I flinched.

You may wonder what I was thinking during all this. I knew this was going to hurt, but I had no fear. My overriding instinct was to get through it and over to the water tub where there would be relief from the pain.

My flinch only caused the spray to bounce from my eye directly into my mouth. I was standing there trying to assess the damage when a wave of heat inflamed my entire face. Surprisingly, my eyes hurt much more than anything else, although I knew I was about to discover a whole new definition of heartburn; I'd swallowed some of the spray. I made my way over to the person holding the strike pad, delivered my three knee blows and was then helped over to the decontamination area. I wanted desperately to keep my face in the nice cool water, but at last I came up for air. I was given a towel and a spray bottle and told to go outside where the fresh cool air offered the fastest recovery. Sounded good, except it was hot outside, the sun was shining, and I'm sure it was the only day I was there that absolutely no breeze was blowing.

We all survived and it was easy to laugh about the experience once our red faces and bloodshot eyes returned to normal. My stomach felt as though I had eaten a plate full of jalapeno peppers, but all in all, I had fared pretty well. It was over. We would not have to experience the burn of pepper spray again—or so we thought. Once back at our dorms, we could not wait to jump in the shower. After a long day, it was just what the doctor ordered. At first I thought the temperature of the shower was too hot, and then I realized what was happening: the water was rinsing the residual pepper spray out of my hair and eyebrows and onto my skin. Women came through this trial in much better shape than men, though. The men who showered later reported that the pepper spray, as well as causing a second burn on their faces, was in their chest hair and made its way down to other parts of their bodies. We women had wondered what all the screaming was about, and now we knew.

―――――

While at Depot, all the troops were exposed to the basics in riot training. We were taught how to march together in formation as we tapped our protective shields with our batons. When done properly, the showing is impressive and achieves the intended effect on a crowd. We also received training in how to move a crowd back using the shields and batons. Specialized units in the RCMP are responsible for this. We cadets received a crash course, which included being subjected to CS gas, also known as tear gas.

Recruits were led to a fairly large room, with an area sectioned off by Plexiglas. Once again I found myself in a situation where I was knowingly going to be inflicted with pain. Here was another "What am I doing?" moment. We were divided into groups, but instead of going in alphabetical order, we went in reverse order this time, so at least I would get it over with quickly (I was Deanna Schmaltz then, filed under S). The instructions going in were as follows: We were to wear our gas masks and then the instructor would call out one of our names. We would then be required to go over to the glass and take off our mask for a short time while the instructor asked questions, and we were expected to respond. The purpose was clear. We would be forced to inhale the tear gas into our lungs, which would cause us to experience burning and other undesirable side effects. Once the instructor was satisfied that we had been exposed (or tortured) enough, that we had a working knowledge of tear gas's effects, we were to *calmly* place our masks back on, take a few breaths and exit the chamber. The chemical in tear gas reacts to moisture in the skin, causing a burning sensation and an involuntary closing of the eyes. Normal reactions include coughing, crying like a baby and having copious amounts of mucus gush out of one's nose.

Now it was my turn. I was wearing our issued grey generic

sweatsuit, straight out of the 1970s. The pants had elastic around the bottom of the legs, which would help keep the tear gas from creeping into sensitive areas of my body. The jacket had a zipper down the front and came with a hood. I cinched the hood up with the strings to make it fit tightly around my face. After suffering the effects of the pepper spray, our action plan was to expose the least amount of skin possible to the tear gas.

The instructor smiled at me and yelled my surname as he had many times before during training. "Schmaltz! You're up! Take your mask off."

I stood up by the glass, smiled and shook my head. This was a little bit about defiance, but it was also about fear.

What was he going to do? Come into a room filled with tear gas and take it off for me? I didn't think so. Not to mention that I really didn't *want* to take my mask off. My instructor was not nearly as amused as I was, but still I saw him flash another smile. Only afterwards did I realize that he was no doubt thinking about what he was going to do to me once I removed my mask. After he provided some more *gentle* encouragement—I think it started with something like, "Schmaltz, if you don't take that mask off . . ."—I reluctantly removed it. It was now payback time for my instructor, and I had a feeling we were going to be there for a while.

He asked me to recite the alphabet in reverse order (I can hardly do it when I'm not under pressure!), then he asked me what my mother's maiden name was, and after that I lost track. My face was already sweaty from the rubber gas mask I'd had on, which only exacerbated the burning sensation. My initial reaction was to hold my breath, which meant that the next breath I took was even deeper, causing the gas to sear my lungs. Then I was coughing and my lungs were on fire.

"Shallow breaths, shallow breaths," my instructor said.

I could hear him but I couldn't see him with tears streaming down my face, and the tears kept coming—just as I had been warned they would. After a few more questions and lots more mucus, I put my mask back on "calmly," took a few breaths of the sweetest gas-mask-canister-produced air I've ever breathed and got out of there. My ordeal was finally over.

For me, the tear gas had been far worse than the pepper spray, even though once I was removed from the gas, everything returned to normal pretty quickly. Even reliving that moment now causes shallow breathing.

The physical and intellectual demands of boot camp paled beside the often degrading rituals of this voluntary confinement. I've already mentioned Bozo Parade and being "busted down" from uniform blues and boots to running shoes and brown pants for this or that infraction. Privilege would be granted, then removed—as if we were children. There was also what was called Piggy Parade. Cadets had to weigh themselves daily, and if our BMI (Body Mass Index) did not match the ideal, the instructor would yell out our names at the beginning of class and we had to respond with our weights. I weighed a mere 122 pounds, and yet somehow I made Piggy Parade. The ritual finally ended when I lost a pound or two and then started to gain from lifting weights. I began to enjoy shouting out my weight, and even the instructor would laugh and shake his head.

Still, at many tasks I excelled. I was the best shot in my troop, which earned me the right to shoot an M16 semi-automatic on the last day at the shooting range. I was also one of the best drivers in my troop. As for the academics, I had already taken most of it in college. I excelled at almost everything, but the lack of privacy and my troop mate snoring two beds down severely tested my limits.

Time passed agonizingly slowly, but finally life at Depot was drawing to an end.

Most of us were dreading our final self-defence class. To pass, we had to participate in a process called "rounds." We were required to fight one of our troop mates using the skills and techniques we had learned over the past several months. Each round lasted for five minutes or until there was a winner. Our instructor gathered everyone and made the announcements for the fights. A few people had dropped out of training, so there was an uneven number of males and females. Two by two the males were paired off, and then two by two the females were paired off, which left me and our male right marker to square off on the mat.

He and I had never really gotten along well. In my humble and juvenile opinion, his leadership skills were lacking. As one of the older cadets, he been appointed to the troop leader position, but he struggled to get us marching correctly, and he did not inspire confidence. I was one of the people who had complained, but I wasn't standing up, raising my hand and begging to take over his duties. I wish now that I had been less critical of his failings and instead had had a part in resolving them. Another lesson learned far too late in life.

The whistle blew. I really don't recall much of the fight because I was in survival mode. My training and instincts kicked in. I do remember, though, that at one point he had my head pinned between his knee and the mat, and it took everything I had to free myself. After what felt like an eternity, the whistle blew again, signalling the end of the fight. A draw. Obviously not as rewarding as a victory, but it sure beat losing! This added to my ten-feet-tall and bulletproof attitude that would in some ways keep me alive in days and years to come. But what goes up must come down.

When I look back on that time, I consider the preparation we had for the work we were about to do and how fine it was—in one way. We acquired the skills we needed; we learned about powers of arrest and taking a statement. All that was a good foundation for police work. But I wish they had prepared us psychologically and emotionally for the cauldron we were about to be dropped into. We had no idea how hot the water would be. In fact, that was a taboo subject. Our instructors were discouraged from telling us war stories.

When a rider gets up on a horse, he or she knows there is a possibility of falling off and suffering a physical injury. The rider is *choosing* to ride the horse knowing what the consequences might be. If you go skydiving, you know there is a chance your parachute won't open and you will plummet to the ground. There are stories out there—stories told to you by a friend, or maybe seen on television. When you sign up to be a police officer, you may understand that there is a possibility you could be killed in the line of duty (an honourable fate for most), but no one tells you about the *psychological* impact or damage of doing the job. These potential consequences are not discussed, thus eliminating your ability to make an informed choice.

As the newest members of the RCMP, we found out a few weeks before graduation where our first postings would be. We had all picked our top three provinces, and we were also able to indicate a preference for what size detachment we preferred: small, medium or large. Ideally, I would be sent to either north-central Alberta or British Columbia, because my fiancé, Jerry Lennox, was in Dawson Creek, British Columbia. We had met in Lethbridge in 1993 while we were both enrolled in the criminal justice program at college. When you joined the RCMP, you were supposed to be prepared to go anywhere in Canada, but times had changed a little. Most people from the eastern provinces were in all likelihood not going back in that direction (that's because Ontario and Quebec have their own provincial police forces, leaving only the Maritimes). But those from British Columbia and Alberta had a good chance of returning to their home provinces.

I was incredibly disappointed to find out that my first detachment was in southern Alberta, only an hour away from my hometown but twelve hours away from Jerry. One of my female troop mates, from Saskatchewan, was sent to Grande Prairie, Alberta—an hour and a half away from my fiancé, and another female troop mate was sent to Fort St. John—only forty-five minutes away from where I wanted to be. She and I made enquiries about switching postings, as it would have suited us both, but the decisions had been made. I had just received my first lesson in the workings of the Royal Canadian Mounted Police, and life was about to get a lot more complicated.

My training came to an end in late August 1996. With friends and family watching, we performed our final parade as a troop, all sharply dressed in our red serge. Afterwards, we packed up our belongings and had our uniforms and equipment shipped to our new detachments. I remember stopping at the gate and videotaping my departure, wondering if one day I would return. Not a chance!

As we moved our boxes out, a new troop was getting ready to move theirs in. Depot is in a constant state of flux. Newly minted Mounties are turned out into the world weekly and new cadets innocently wander in to take their place.

On my way home, I flipped open my badge six or seven times just to make sure it was real. It was, and remains, a symbol of one of the biggest accomplishments in my life, and that day I was truly a proud Mountie. In that sense, the training had done what it set out to do: it had instilled in me a pride in the institution and in the uniform. With my rose-coloured glasses firmly in place, I set off to make the world a better place.

CHAPTER THREE

The Eyes of a Horse

My daughter, Skylar, wanted desperately to take horseback riding lessons. This was in 2007, when she was five. I found a stable close to where we lived and signed her up. Because of her age, I had to participate in the class and lead the horse around the arena while Skylar sat on his back and learned the basics of riding. I didn't grow up owning horses, but as a girl visiting rural relations in Saskatchewan I had ridden many times either on trail rides or at the farms of friends and family. I'd play tag with cousins on horseback. Western saddles, no instruction. You just climbed aboard and did it.

My deeper affinity for horses would come later in life, but a bond with animals was rooted in my childhood. My family had always had dogs. In 2012, I had to have Lucy—my twelve-year-old retriever cross—put down. She had developed liver cancer and I was there at the end when she got the lethal injection. That was one of the hardest things I have ever done. For many years, time alone with Lucy had been my source of comfort.

We have two dogs now, including a young black Greyhound named Sam, rescued from the dog track world. I have seen the video that shows him breaking a leg bone during a race, an incident that finished his career as a professional runner. Still, Sam is lightning fast. It's a thrill to watch his sleek form take off in pursuit of a ball at the park near our house.

And there's Neo, a shar-pei who famously (in my family at least) got lost during a family reunion in rural Alberta and in so doing gave me insight into something I had already experienced as a police officer—hypervigilance. This was in 2010 when I had been in the force some fourteen years. Everyone at the reunion was camping in a large field outside a community recreation centre in a hamlet in south-central Alberta. It was dark and nearing midnight when a few members of the younger generation announced they had some fireworks and proceeded to set them off. Jerry and I immediately went back to the trailer we were borrowing for the weekend to check on the dogs. Lucy was exactly where we had left her, but Neo was nowhere to be seen. He had managed to climb out of the kennel and slip underneath the surrounding tent-like shelter we had set up. We spent the next few hours searching for him in the dark but with no success. He was only eight months old at the time.

We set out again early the next morning and discovered a large hole in the chain-link fence behind the field. Further inspection led to paw prints in the dirt—now we had a direction of travel. Unfortunately, Neo's chosen path led to the outskirts of town and into the bush. Finding him would be like finding the proverbial needle in the haystack.

Partway through the day, we stopped to talk to a farmer

who was parked on the side of one of the back roads. He mentioned that he had seen a dog in the field with his cows earlier that morning. As I walked along the road toward the field, I saw another farmer driving a tractor and was going to ask him if he'd seen a dog in the area, when up popped Neo onto the road. I felt such overwhelming joy. I called out to him in disbelief that we had actually found him. But he looked at me and took off running underneath a barbwire fence into a field of trees and bushes.

We ran after him, pried apart the horizontal barbed wires in a fence to jump through and stayed with him for a time, only to lose him again in the tall brush. We were devastated. He was just a puppy, after all, and with all the coyotes, foxes and animals out there, he had somehow managed to survive the night—but now we had lost him for the second time.

Neo made an appearance two more times, but dashed back into hiding whenever we got near him. It crossed my mind that maybe he wanted to be free. Why else would he run away from us?

Unknowingly, we had herded him into an area near a creek. Neo was not a water dog and would do anything to avoid it. Jerry was continuing to push forward, scanning his surroundings, when he heard a noise. He looked behind him and spotted Neo hiding in the bush. Neo must have caught Jerry's scent as he walked by, and that snapped the dog out of the state he was in. He finally "recognized" Jerry. When Jerry turned around and called, our pup came running into his arms.

Why would the dog who loves us—and who was no doubt distraught at being separated from us—run from us? Later on, a veterinarian explained to us the phenomenon of "hysterical blindness":

the dog's fear at being lost and separated meant that, temporarily at least, he could not recognize his own "pack," or family.

I couldn't help but compare this case of hysterical blindness with a term commonly used in law enforcement called "hyper-vigilance"—being in a constant state of alertness. Everyone and everything is perceived as a threat or an enemy. My initial reaction to Neo's behaviour was to assume that he preferred to be alone. I never considered the possibility that he felt so threatened and so scared that he was stuck in a pattern of believing that everyone and everything around him was going to hurt him. He didn't really want to be alone. All he wanted was for someone to open up their arms and take him home. The only thing that shifted Neo out of his fight–flight response was his sense of smell. He needed to get out of his head and trust his body—only then could he find home.

———

Just seeing Skylar ride ignited something in me. I started taking riding lessons from the same stable where she had learned.

I had quit playing soccer by that point. I had played it for most of my life and yet I couldn't find the passion for it anymore. What I would have once considered competitiveness in other players, I now perceived as combativeness. In my hypervigilant state, that aggression triggered my fight-or-flight response, and I was in a place where I wanted to fight. I wanted to react. I wanted to hurt people. Hurting them made me feel good temporarily, releasing the rage that had been brewing inside for so long. But soccer, an activity that once gave me joy, now just made me angry and frustrated. My conscience always kicked in and made me feel ashamed and disgusted that I couldn't control myself. I didn't have the coping strategies to deal with my anger, so I quit playing altogether.

When I came into contact with the horses, something within me sparked. Just being around them put me back in touch with a sense of passion that I hadn't felt in a long time. It was the first time since the beginning of my policing career that I had felt something other than anger. What came of that experience was the desire to have a horse of my own.

In 2008, my friend Shelley, an experienced horse owner, agreed to help me. She was happy to shop around and came along on a few occasions to test-drive horses to find a good fit for me. I didn't want to admit to myself or anyone else that I was a "green" rider— one with little or no experience—in fact, fluorescent green! But Shelley found a quarter horse palomino at a farm not too far away. I've always adored palomino horses, so we went to see her. She was a mare named Maggie, and she was absolutely beautiful. My first ride on her wasn't perfect: she refused to stop when I asked her to. But I was convinced that she was the horse for me. We loaded her up in the trailer, and I handed over the cheque.

The owner suggested I take her on a trial basis. If it didn't work out, I could bring her back, no problem. Maggie started whinnying and stomping in the trailer (naturally, for she was being removed from her home herd and territory), and I must have looked like I was ready to unload her and forget the whole idea. Shelley hustled me into the truck, and we headed back to her farm.

The logical part of my brain was saying "No!" but the rest of me was ready for an adventure.

All I knew was that sitting on Maggie's back I felt awake for the first time in a long time. I can't quite explain it. Was I blinded by her beauty? Is that what compelled me to buy her? Perhaps. There was an irrational, impulsive element to the decision that was uncharacteristic of my well-thought-out and logical way of approaching life. I had typically spent most of my time in my head. The constant and often repetitive thoughts cycled through my mind over and over and yes, Maggie was beautiful, but she also represented a sense of stillness and quiet that I longed for. And in that silence, I heard this whisper of joy. I could even over-look the danger.

And danger there was. While on a trail ride with Shelley on one of her horses, in 2008, our mounts had been spooked by a moose, and my horse bolted. On another ride, this time near Elk Island National Park, Shelley's horse shied at a branch on the trail and the horse fell, with Shelley pinned underneath. She suffered a broken nose and damage to one leg, still an issue for her today.

In the months after Maggie became mine, several things hap-pened. First, I came to understand a new kind of friendship. My philosophy on friendship had always been this: Don't ask me to do anything for you, and I won't ask you to do anything for me. You stay there and I'll stay here. We can converse, but I really don't want to know the details of your life, and please don't expect me to tell you the details about my life. I'm completely open to having fun, but fun on a superficial level.

Shelley helped me learn how to ride and handle my new mare, but being the way I was, I didn't like being dependent on her. I felt inadequate having to ask her for help all the time, even though I knew she didn't mind, and in fact, she enjoyed it. At one point she had to go away for a few days and asked if I would come out to her place in the country and take care of the horses. Me? She had helped me so much that I felt obligated to take on the job. I drove out in the morning, checked on all the horses and fed them, and did it all again that evening. Maybe this give-and-take thing wasn't so bad after all.

My friendship with Shelley was really the first step in coming out of an isolation I'd been feeling due to my job and my related depression and workplace injuries. I never wanted to get too close to any one person because I didn't want them to ask me about what I did for a living. I didn't want to lie, but I wasn't willing to tell the truth either. The easiest thing to do was to keep to myself and not let anyone too close. But the more time I spent with Shelley, the more I enjoyed her company and, most of all, her friendship. My world was growing bigger.

The second thing that happened was that I realized my horse hated me. Well, *hate* might be a little dramatic, but I had the strong feeling that if given the choice, she would choose not to be in my presence.

Grooming Maggie, for example, was an issue. She would move—step to the side, forwards or backwards—a split second before the brush touched her. While I was leading her, she would try to race ahead. Her previous owner had been a farrier (a specialist in hoof care), and Maggie was quite comfortable having her feet picked up so I could clean her hooves. But I was decidedly uncomfortable performing this task. I was on high alert, and of course I conveyed my nervousness to her.

Shelley and I went for a ride one nice day during the winter. I had never ridden in snow before, and I was looking forward to a winter wonderland experience. We rode down the long driveway and crossed the road into a field. Maggie kept putting her head down and acting strangely. She wasn't being her usual high-headed, excited self and seemed lethargic. Next thing I knew, her knees buckled. She was going to roll—with me on her back! I managed to get my feet out of the stirrups and threw myself off to the side as she went down. We both got back on our feet, shook off the snow and looked at each other. Hers was a look of complete satisfaction, and mine was one of shock. This is apparently an old pony trick: some will drop and roll to ditch the youngster on their backs. It may sound odd, but I am thankful to Maggie that she chose the gentler method of putting me on the ground. Bucking, bolting or rearing would have done the job just as effectively but could have caused me a lot more pain.

I had been battling the RCMP on several fronts at that point, and the last thing I needed was another fight on my hands. I had bought a horse because I wanted to be able to go out, saddle her up and take long and relaxing rides in the company of my friend. I wanted an easy and enjoyable horse to take my mind off everything else that was going on. But like everything else, it just wasn't going to be that simple. The more time we spent together, the more Maggie and I became frustrated with each other. I felt like she had come to me in a good state of mind and now I was "wrecking" her. I may have been a rank amateur as a horse trainer, but this much I knew: my horse felt an antipathy toward me. I watched Maggie with other riders and trainers at horse clinics, and she was always a dream with them. Even with green riders, she was a sweet horse. With me, she just got progressively worse. Of course, the problem was not Maggie. The problem was me.

My choices were to sell her or to figure out this whole horse thing. I was never one to take the easy road, so I decided on the latter option. I had no idea that my time spent trying to understand Maggie would give me great insight into understanding myself.

———

The eyes of a horse are not the biggest in the animal kingdom; there is a giant squid with eyes the size of dinner plates. But I doubt that any other animal on the planet has eyes so expressive.

In her book *Dark Horses and Black Beauties*, American author Melissa Holbrook Pierson describes in exquisite prose what draws us to the horse. "So it is first," she writes, "the way they look, both to and at us, that pins us flat. It is a magisterial beauty . . . They are a stirringly impossible mixture of power and delicacy, size and fragility. They inspire fear even as they are filled with it themselves. They are wild and they are utterly tamable." Pierson finally writes of a horse's eyes—"great pools of assessment and expression"—that she is convinced they pull us in, appealing at some deep and primitive level to a human desire to nurture.

First responders who have been damaged in their work sometimes have difficulty grasping the concept of horses as agents of change. Horses themselves don't heal people; connecting with horses is what heals. The horses enable the connection because they are safe (I don't mean that horses can't harm a human, but rare is the horse who *intends* harm), they are nonjudgmental and they respond differently and immediately as you change within yourself. As you become more connected to yourself, you open the door for connection to the horse.

People seem constantly to be looking for some *outside* force to bring them peace or to heal their wounds. The horse serves as a reminder that the answers come from within. They act as a mirror and allow you to see certain patterns in your behaviour when you become stressed. When you identify what those behaviours are and make changes, the results in the horse—and you—are immediate and undeniable.

Working with horses is special because humans have to adjust and rethink—on the fly. We are predators; they are prey. It's much easier for a predator to relate to a predator, human to dog, for example. To work with horses is to tap into one's vulnerability. We are human, top of the food chain. For many humans, and especially first responders, *vulnerability* is a dirty word.

To achieve balance, though, we must not only look at our prey side—or our intuitive side—but embrace it. We are conditioned to believe that vulnerability equates with weakness. Nothing could be further from the truth.

The horse is a living creature, but in one way the horse is like a machine—a biofeedback machine. When you are one-on-one with a horse, that horse will mirror your emotions and respond accordingly. How well I now know this to be true. The horse is extremely sensitive to stress and fear; it can read such emotions in our bodies. An angry or fearful human will repel a horse, but a horse will follow any human worthy of that horse's trust. Sounds simple. It's not.

CHAPTER FOUR

New Recruit

My first posting—in Brooks, southeastern Alberta—was a medium-sized detachment in a town with a population of about thirteen thousand. I had about a week between graduation and starting my new post. As I was decompressing at my parents' house and getting organized for the start of my new career, I received a call from my new detachment commander. He explained that the detachment was short on members and asked if I could start work there a few days early. Early meant the next day on night shift. He would pay for me to stay at a local hotel for a few nights, and then I could drive back to gather my belongings and move into my new apartment. I was eager to start and wondered what it was going to be like.

On my very first shift, I went to a call and encountered a man who had just had his throat slashed. So began my life lessons in the human condition, in the summer of 1996.

Despite its small size, several factors made Brooks a busy place to work as a police officer. The town had lots of young people and an extremely diverse ethnic population. And because of the flourishing oil patch, many residents had money—which led to issues with drugs and alcohol and the violence that tends to follow.

As a new recruit, my first six months were spent in the Recruit Field Training (RFT) program. I was assigned to a senior member, a mentor, who was required to monitor my files and basic job competencies. Some coaches have a true interest in starting the recruit off on the right foot, while others see it as an opportunity to slough off their files. I started my training with a member who had just trained several other recruits and didn't seem really keen to take on another. Still, he did his best to muster up some enthusiasm, and he did what was required to get me through my probation period.

After a few short weeks, I was unleashed into the Brooks community in my own police cruiser. Many people mistakenly believe that the RCMP operates as many municipal police forces do—with two officers in one car out on patrol. But in the RCMP, and especially in small and medium-sized detachments, an officer on patrol operates alone more often than not. At night and at certain times during the day or on weekends, I was alone at the detachment. There was no on-site dispatcher. The calls were routed right to my car.

My heart would skip a beat every time the communication radio beeped to announce a call. I remember driving downtown and seeing myself reflected in store windows as I passed. How odd: to catch a glimpse of yourself as others see you. I remember this as a moment of pride and confirmation. The person in the reflection was me, and what I was doing was real.

The inside of a police car looks like a cross between the cockpit of an airplane and the inside of a tank. Looking in from the outside, you see an array of buttons and switches along with briefcases and other equipment the officer may need during a shift. Most police vehicles are also equipped with a laptop, through which calls from the communication centre come in. A police car looks like organized chaos with not much room to spare.

While on duty, I was supposed to wear a forage cap—flat on the top, with a yellow band bearing the RCMP crest, and a visor. (In fact, I seldom wore the hat because it wouldn't go over my ponytail.) I wore a short-sleeve grey shirt and, underneath it, my soft body-armour vest. Several months later, this body armour would be replaced with an external carrier that slipped over my head and strapped around my torso. I wore navy blue pants with yellow stripes down each side, and at my waist was a heavily laden belt on which hung my firearm, spare magazines, radio, pepper spray and expandable baton. Finally, I had on my black workboots. Polished, of course.

I started each shift by lugging my heavy briefcase to the front passenger seat of the car. Inside that briefcase was all the paperwork I could ever imagine I might need while on patrol. My metal ticket case and metal notebook holder were also in there, providing a hard surface on which to write tickets or take a statement during the course of my duties. I would throw it in the front seat and belt it in so it didn't go flying and dump the contents all over the vehicle while I was in pursuit of someone or something—it only takes forgetting to secure the seat belt once to learn that lesson.

I can close my eyes now and see everything. I open the driver's side door and slide myself behind the wheel. I smell that pungent odour of stale alcohol lingering from someone who had been intoxicated in the back seat. With my left hand, I reach down and find the seat adjustment buttons. The seat creaks and groans as I demand it come all the way to the top of its settings and a little bit forward. As I adjust the rear-view mirror, the partition that separates the back seat from the front seat (often referred to as the silent patrolman) comes into my view. The top portion is made of Plexiglas with a small sliding window in the middle. I push the spring-loaded button and slide the window over to the closed position. The button pops up and I hear the pin lock in place. It's easier to open it if it's needed than to try to close it when someone is going ballistic in the back.

I slide the key into the ignition, turn it over and listen as the V8 engine roars to life. The vehicle's modifications make it more durable and stable. I can feel the power underneath and around me, but what I'm aware of most is the heaviness. I know this Ford Crown Victoria can travel 220 kilometres per hour because I've made it go that fast on the highway during a high-speed pursuit. I am also aware, however, of how loaded down the car is with all the equipment in the cab and trunk. The car feels commanding, but more safe than fast.

Now, with the engine on, the radio and all the lights flicker as they are awakened to start my shift. On the dash, stuffed off to the left corner, is the radar unit. I need to remember to take the tuning forks out of the cubbyhole in the door and calibrate the unit if I plan on writing any speeding tickets. All the buttons, flips and switches are off to my right—within easy access. The controls for the red and blue overhead lights, the spotlights and the siren are on the same black box. The other part of the radar unit, which displays the speed of oncoming vehicles, is located a bit higher, where the AM/FM radio sits. Lower, closer to the floor, the radio beeps as it turns on. I notice the hard and cold metal against my right leg and take note of the shotgun.

It's secured in a metal holder that's pointed toward the floor. The safety is on and the clamp has it secured in its proper place. I reach over with my right hand and pull the seat belt over my bulky Kevlar vest and find the buckle hiding underneath my sidearm attached to my gun belt. I step on the brake and slide the transmission into drive. My steel partner and I are ready to head out onto the streets.

***

During those first months while I was stumbling my way through the ins and outs of different calls (not to mention trying to get the paperwork straight), another member at the detachment took it upon herself to teach me how to survive—both on the street and as a member of the organization. Sue had about nine years' service when I met her. She was already tired and a little bitter, but she was extremely street smart and she liked her job like nobody I've ever seen. Sue used to say, "I may not know much, but I know people," and she certainly did. She had a knack for knowing ahead of time what people were going to do or say—and I wanted that ability too. With her, my real training started.

I was like a sponge. I wanted to know more, see more, and find answers to all the questions I had ever had about people and what made them do the things they do. I volunteered for every overtime shift, and when I wasn't in uniform in a police car, I was in a police car as a ride-along in civilian clothes. Sue would pick me up from home during the night, and I would drive around with her until I had my fill. I lived and breathed my job. My only other activity was going to the gym in between shifts.

Sue's teaching style was painful yet effective. When I went on shift with her during this training period, she believed in giving me as much rope as I needed, and she would only step in to "save me" if I was about to make a mistake that would result in severe consequences. The rest she called "learning experiences"—and there were many. She only had to save me a few times, but she never lets me forget one night when we were riding together and we received a complaint about a possible impaired driver on a back road near town.

I was driving, and Sue was in the passenger seat. Impaired files are actually one of the more complex ones because of the paperwork involved; particular elements need to be addressed to lay a successful charge. We located the vehicle, and I pulled in behind and observed the person's driving, which was slow and anything but in a straight line. I activated my lights and sirens. The vehicle made its way over to the right shoulder. I strategically positioned my police car in behind, and I had a brief conversation with Sue, who reminded me of what steps I needed to follow. She said she would come to the driver's side and watch and listen.

I exited my car, approached the vehicle and engaged the female driver in conversation to help establish if she had been drinking. Then I looked back somewhat anxiously for my partner, who was nowhere to be found. Sue finally appeared and walked toward me. I gave her a "where were you?" look, and she pointed to her clothes as she brushed grass and thistle from her uniform. Not understanding, I returned to dealing with the female driver and ended up arresting her and placing her in the back seat of our police car.

Sue later let me in on what had taken her so long. In the dark, I had apparently pulled over too far onto the shoulder, beside a drop-off, and when she stepped out of the police car, she went down. Mistake number one: dumping your backup and trainer in a ditch.

Mistake number two would soon follow. On our way back to the detachment, I looked in the rear-view mirror to check on the woman, and I couldn't see her. Where had she gone? Were the windows down, and had she climbed out? How had I managed to lose a *person*? What was I going to tell Sue? Inside my head, I was having a meltdown. Trying to remain calm, I looked back over my shoulder again, and in a moment of intense relief, I saw the top of the woman's head.

I was confused until I remembered that earlier in the night, someone had vomited in the back seat. The seat is removable, and I had taken it out in the bay at the detachment to wash it and had forgotten to put it back in. The woman I'd arrested, who was less than five feet tall, was sitting on the floor. Note to self: reassemble the back seat of the police car before responding to another call.

———

Over the next eighteen months, Sue and I found ourselves in a variety of situations together—a good mix of highly productive police work and fun. When we get together now, we reminisce mostly about the good times.

One afternoon we received a call concerning a hay bale that had fallen off a truck and was blocking one lane of the Trans-Canada Highway. We headed out thinking we'd scrape a few flakes of hay off the road—and arrived to find an enormous round bale weighing a thousand pounds or more. We looked in the trunk of the police car and all we could find was a shovel and a broom. Picking up hay with a shovel is like picking up water with a fork. Nevertheless, we worked feverishly, and fruitlessly, to push the hay off the highway until the highway maintenance truck came.

Sue stared at me oddly and asked if I was okay. She said I sounded short of breath and didn't look well. A glance at my arms revealed that I was covered in hives, and I was indeed having trouble catching my breath. She told me my face was red and blotchy. I have always had hay fever, but I didn't know I was allergic to *hay*.

Sue drove me to the hospital, where a nurse prepared to give me a shot. As I sheepishly rolled up my sleeve, I heard the dreaded words, "Not in your arm." How uncool to be a cop in uniform and have to take off your gun belt, drop your pants and stand there while a nurse gives you a needle in the butt. I looked to my trusted trainer for rescue, but all I got was a giggle, and her expression said, *It's happening with or without your co-operation. You decide.*

I consider Sue a great friend, and in fact, we often refer to ourselves as sisters, but I learned early on—don't mess with her. So I did as I was told. Later, Sue drove me to a doctor's office, where I experienced a little dizziness and almost fell over. That's the last thing I remember, other than Sue covering me up with a blanket and bundling me home to my couch. I haven't lived that one down either.

———

Sue taught me well and she helped me to develop the skills I needed to be successful in the job, but she also passed on an unspoken way of being that would keep me relatively unharmed. It was about exuding confidence and fearlessness and about commanding respect simply by one's demeanour. We were in the local bar one night doing a check. Inside, a bad character with a long history of violence was playing pool with his buddies. He was well-known to police.

He walked within a respectable distance of my partner and said, "Would you fight me, Sue?"

Without missing a beat, she responded, "To the death."

They stared at each other, just briefly, and he turned to his friends and said, "See, that's why I respect her."

I find it hard to explain the significance and the intensity of that moment, even for me as a bystander, but I will never forget it.

I've had conversations with colleagues about the concept of sheep and wolves—that is, who are the predators and who are the prey in society. I'll always remember a story Jerry told me once that stuck with me. He was standing outside a bar and someone he knew from school was there with friends. This man had a criminal history and one of his favourite hobbies was fighting. He had been kicked out of the bar, and it was time for last call. The doors would be opening soon as a signal for everyone to leave. Jerry heard him yell across the street to the bouncers, "Let out the sheep!"

These "wolves" have a talent for picking out the vulnerable, whether by a look in someone's eye or the way they walk. I believe it boils down to some sort of unconscious ability to detect the slightest degree of insecurity, weakness or fear in another person. This explains the stare-down during that bar check. The guy could detect no weakness in Sue, which is why she passed his little test. Why is it important to have the "respect" of a bad guy? What does that mean? Next time there's a bar fight or trouble, that guy may not help you, but he may not jump you either.

What I didn't understand then is that one can't "learn" to be a wolf; one has to "become" a wolf. A wolf can be a wolf in sheep's clothing, but a sheep can't be a sheep in wolf's clothing. You can con a sheep, but a wolf knows a wolf. There is no faking, no pretending.

Sue and I spent time together both on duty and off. We worked hard and we played hard. Often on the same page and thinking the same thing without having to say it out loud, we were, and still are, alike in many ways.

All members of the detachment were responsible for policing not only the main community but also several towns and villages located in our detachment area. There were designated "rural" members of the RCMP, but municipal officers, too, often attended calls in the rural areas. One night a call came in about a domestic dispute in one of the smaller communities about twenty minutes away. Sue and I were working and jumped in a car together and drove out. We knew of the couple involved. The male, in particular, was known to be violent and didn't care much for the police.

We arrived at the residence and got out of the car to walk to the door, stopping for a moment outside to listen and see if we could determine what was going on and who was where in the house. We heard screaming. Both Sue and I had the same reaction and burst through the door. In the hallway, two people were on the ground fighting—but not the husband and wife. The wife was astride her preadolescent daughter, who was lying on her back. The woman hadn't heard us come in the house because she was too focused on what she was doing—beating her child. As she cocked her fist back to deliver another blow, Sue and I tackled her.

We picked her up and escorted her outside, placed her under arrest and put her in the police car. By then, a third RCMP officer had arrived on the scene, and she went inside. Sue and I knew we needed to get back inside as soon as possible to make sure our colleague wasn't in trouble. We re-entered the residence to find her with the husband—who was also the father of the girl—in the living room, where all was calm. This man was quite happy that *he* wasn't the one going to jail for a change. We were leery about breaking the news that we would be required to contact Social Services, who would have to come out and assess the situation, but his euphoria over not going to jail seemed to overcome any potential anger.

We eventually left the scene and started the drive back to town, where the female would be booked into cells and charged with assault. As we drove away, it must have clicked that she was going to jail. Her hands were handcuffed behind her back, so she proceeded to bang her head against the Plexiglas. We ignored her temper tantrum, so she decided to turn it up a couple of notches. She used all the force she could muster, smashing her head on the partition. The blood from her nose started to flow. I was shocked. I'd never seen anything like it.

It wouldn't be the last time in my career that I would see self-inflicted injury, but this first one made an unsettling impression. Sue was driving, and she pulled over to the side of the road. In her best "don't mess" voice, she told the woman that if she didn't knock it off, we would hog-tie her. The woman said a few words back that don't bear repeating, but when we set off again, the banging stopped, and the rest of the ride back to the detachment was uneventful.

Social Services was contacted, and all the children in the house were removed and placed into temporary care. Sometime later, I accompanied a social worker to the residence. She was doing a follow-up visit and wanted a police presence there in case the couple became agitated about not having their children returned that day. I remember the social worker telling me that the two parents had some work to do, but the children would be returned to the home at some point in the near future. It all just seemed so wrong, but it was completely out of my hands.

Many shifts were challenging, but some calls were absolute chaos, with no time to make sense of anything. One bar in town had earned a reputation for after-hours fighting in the parking lot. I had gone there or to the adjoining field on several occasions to discover more than one person lying unconscious after a fight. Some brawls involved fifty or more people—and a handful of Mounties pulling up to save the day. It was crazy.

Occasionally local residents would put up posters advertising "Newfie Night." Some Newfoundlanders had found work at the local meat-packing plant—jobs that almost no one else wanted. The plant also recruited ex-convicts as well as Somalis and Filipinos, people whose homelands were rife with civil war and unrest. The work in the slaughterhouse had its own horrors and impacts. Imagine the tensions when all these folks gathered; now imagine them drunk or on drugs.

One night several of us were on the scene, and a female and her boyfriend were arrested and placed in one of the police cars. We were dealing with another fight when I heard the distinct sound of breaking glass. The male had kicked out the side window of the police car and was trying to get out. I ran over to grab him, and another member managed to get one handcuff on him before the guy pulled away and tried to run. I pushed him up against a car and saw the handcuff dangling from his left wrist. I focused on that arm because if I got hit in the face with a handcuff it would cause serious damage. As I attempted to restrain his left arm, he wound up with his right arm and punched me square in the face. I didn't flinch. I grabbed him and, with the help of an auxiliary member, pulled him to the ground. (Auxiliary members are volunteers who receive training but carry no firearms.)

By then, other members were able to help me place the handcuffs on him properly and put him in a different police car. My nose was sore, but I didn't pay much attention. On a busy night, there wasn't much time to rest between calls. Adrenaline and a hint of ego prevented me from getting any medical attention, but that fist to the face eventually resulted in a permanent bump on the side of my nose. There's a life lesson in there somewhere.

Another bar that kept us busy was known locally as "The Zoo." One afternoon we received a call to attend the place. The disturbance appeared to be over, and we—two other officers and I—were standing outside the back door of the building. I was by my car, leaning against the front near the driver's side door. We were talking among ourselves when the back door of the bar opened and a male exited. I stood up, but I didn't recognize the person (he hadn't been involved in the previous fracas) and wasn't planning to pay him any more attention, but he had something else in mind. He walked up to me, pushed me against the police car and said, "Better luck next time," then took off.

The chase was on. I could clearly see him running down the middle of the alley, and I took off after him. Another officer gave chase as well, but he was near the end of his service and liked his Slurpees from 7-Eleven. I suddenly saw his expandable baton go flying by my head, and I heard him yell from behind me, "Throw yours too, D!" I was waiting for a boot or something else to come next! But I didn't need to throw anything. I was in the best shape of my life, and I was angry. My quarry had started off strong, but he petered out by the end of the block. He turned in to the front yard of a residence, and when I caught up to him, there we stood, face to face. Refusing to get down on the ground, he came at me.

He had put his hands on me once before, so I had already taken out my pepper spray. I gave him one shot directly in the eyes. This is the moment when the person usually drops to the ground swearing in pain. This guy stopped in his tracks, but then he reached up with his hand and wiped the spray from his eyes and smiled. No effect whatsoever. We were told in training at

Depot that a very small portion of the population does not react to pepper spray. This guy happened to be one of them.

We were in a standoff, and he was still not listening. Luckily, I had my baton, and I was ready to use it if he was determined to continue down this path. And then I heard it—the sweet sound of a Crown Victoria engine screaming down the alley. A third officer was soon skidding to a stop right behind me. Funny how numbers can make people's attitudes change. The runner was now ready to listen, and I arrested him without further incident. He was charged with assaulting a police officer.

No two days in the life of a police officer are ever the same. In Brooks, I might have been sent on two calls one day and ten the next. But always, sitting on my desk were files in various stages of completion. That was the one constant: paperwork. Most calls don't end in that moment of drama. It's like being a dishwasher in a restaurant; the job has no beginning or end. Many of my files involved serious offences and were demanding as far as paperwork goes.

The attending officer always had to take statements, and sometimes other parties had to be chased down for these. I was always pursuing someone. Then I had to prepare "court packages"—one for the prosecutor, one for the defence. In the old days, I had to wrestle with a photocopier. One ten-hour shift might generate a pile of documents measuring three or four inches thick. There's no other word for it. The paperwork was *nasty*.

As time went on, I got better at it. I learned to write files more quickly, and to prioritize. Paperwork was often boring and

I could get lost in it, but then the phone would ring and out the door I would go to another call. It might be something as innocuous as two neighbours squabbling over a barking dog or as menacing as a man in a bar with a butcher knife.

I learned to switch gears in a hurry. Even then, as a rookie cop, I knew this much: complacency kills.

———

So much happened during those first couple of years, and now, as I cast through my memories, I can't help but notice that the lighthearted ones come to mind first. But it wasn't always good times.

One afternoon when I was working by myself, I received a call about a male who had driven his vehicle through a chain-link fence to get into a factory along the Trans-Canada Highway about 25 kilometres away. He had stolen some items, loaded up his car and tried to flee the scene. But crashing through the fence had effectively disabled his car, so he had run off into an adjacent field. He was wearing, the radio dispatcher said, a dark blue shirt and blue jeans. I headed out to the scene and en route asked Dispatch if they could call the member who was coming in later and ask him to start rolling for backup. I knew that Dispatch would have to call him at home, that he would have to don his uniform, drive to the detachment, put on his gun belt and body armour, grab a police car and head out to the scene. He was going to be at least half an hour, so for now I was on my own.

When I arrived at the scene, I observed the car with the hood slammed up against the windshield, and in the middle of the field of light brown grass, a man matching the description I had been given. He wasn't hard to spot. Just to make things interesting, I had lost radio contact with Dispatch, and there was no cellphone service. It is a common assumption that our equipment is top-of-the-line, but the reality can be quite different. I had reached the outer limits of my detachment boundaries, so there was no coverage and I lost radio contact. I had entered a communications dead spot. Worse, an employee from the plant had advised Dispatch that there were guns on the premises, but no one was available to confirm whether or not any had been taken by the fellow lying in the field. A perfect storm was brewing.

I approached the male, who was lying on his stomach with his hands hidden under his chest. I estimated that he was about six foot four, with a slim build. With my gun out and by my side, I told him that I was a police officer and that I needed to see his hands immediately.

His response was less than co-operative. He was obviously agitated and a little unstable. All I wanted was to see his hands. He could lie there all day long if he wanted to, but for my own safety I needed to see what he was hiding underneath his body. If things went wrong, I was in the middle of nowhere, with no radio or phone service. Backup was still a good half hour away, and lots can happen in that time. I asked him again to show me his hands, and he became more agitated, swearing at me and telling me he was going to kill me. I told him that he was mistaken if he thought I wouldn't shoot him, and he looked at me and said, "Then why are your fuckin' hands shaking?"

To my surprise and dismay, I noticed that he was right—and it angered me. The only way I was going to get out of this situation alive, he told me, was if I killed him first. Time slowed down, and inside my head I can still hear a loud click. It wasn't a gun or weapon; it was a door in my mind suddenly closing. During those rookie years, I had thought about whether or not I could kill someone if I had to protect myself or someone else, and I had always felt deep down that I could. It's different, though, when you're faced with that decision and you *know* what the answer is.

The answer was yes. Yes, I could shoot this person. Yes, I could end his life if it meant saving mine.

I was forever changed in that moment.

He continued to yell and threaten me, and then something else became clear: He was trying to get me to shoot him, a ploy known as "suicide by cop." He wasn't afraid of me shooting him. In fact, he was doing everything he could think of to make me angry enough to pull the trigger. That's what he wanted, and that's what he had been trying to tap into all along.

The situation was escalating, yet I felt calm. I knew I could pull the trigger and didn't have to think about it anymore. But knowing I could do it made me *not* want to do it. I needed to change tactics. I told him that I didn't want to shoot him and that obviously he was having a really bad day. By this time, he was becoming more animated, and he had moved his hands. I could see that he didn't have any weapons. I holstered my gun and elected for my baton in one hand and pepper spray in the other. I was telling him to put his hands behind his back, and he looked like he was going to co-operate, when suddenly he got onto his knees.

I knew if he stood up, my advantage would be lost. I needed to act while he was still on the ground. I jumped on him and pinned him down, managing to handcuff him. And then it hit me. The anger. I was angry that he had put me in that situation, angry that he had threatened to kill me—angry on some level I wasn't even able to comprehend at the time. I somehow managed to swallow that feeling, got him into the car and drove him back to the detachment.

I sat down with him in an interview room and did what I needed to do and said what I needed to say to get him to open up and explain what had just happened. He had had a fight with his girlfriend, and he had started drinking. He had gotten into his car and started to drive. He had seen the plant on the side of the road and rammed the chain-link fence. He had stolen some computer equipment, then run into the field and waited for the police to arrive. During his confession, he stated that he had wanted to die and had tried to use me as a means to his end.

Police officers have these experiences often—without being given the time or skills to process what has happened. We force ourselves to stuff it down deep in the name of professionalism. The encounter in the field had rocked me to my core. It had been a pivotal moment for me, and before I was able to process it, I was sitting across from this man oozing with empathy so he would confess and explain everything he had done.

I remember the first time I sat across from a pedophile who had molested several young children. To extract a confession, I forced myself to empathize with him and make him feel like I understood how he could find young girls sexually attractive. After the interview I sat in the bathroom and thought I was going to throw up. I quickly learned to train myself to be numb, to separate myself from what was actually happening.

We do what we do for the "greater good," but it takes a toll on our hearts and our souls. Police officers and first responders, in general, have a history of trying to numb it out using alcohol or drugs. Unless you deal with the feelings, they never go away, and they weave destruction into our lives through depression, addictions, anxiety and, of course, anger.

It wasn't a conscious decision, but I soon embarked on a path that used anger as a way to plug any openings where weakness might show through. At the time, it's what I needed to do to survive. It makes me sad to write this now. It marked the beginning of what looked to be the end: the end of innocence, the end of joy and the end of hope. In hindsight, I was riding the crest of a wave before the epic trough. I was flying from one call to the next, soaking in the experiences, but moving too fast and having too much "fun" to bother dealing with the emotions along the way. This strategy would eventually catch up to me, but not for a while. For now, I was ten feet tall and bulletproof.

———

Sue was my mentor, the one who gave me a great head-start, teaching me much of what I needed to know about life as a cop. I became a student of what I thought was "real life." The interview room became the greatest classroom of all.

I remember interviewing a young guy about some break and enters that had occurred in town. I don't recall how I came up with his name, but he agreed to come to the detachment and be interviewed. I had just read a book about interviewing, and I was eager to try out some new techniques. I sat down in a chair next to him and began the process by telling him that I knew he had done it. To my surprise, he gave it up right away, and I thought to myself, Hey, this stuff really works! I was speechless for a moment, and he said that he couldn't just give me everything right off the bat and wanted me at least to ask him some questions. I thought it was the greatest thing.

I enjoyed interviewing people, especially suspects, and I read as much material about interviewing as I could find and watched other members as I worked hard to develop my own style of getting people to open up. I found it easy—in part because I was truly interested in people's stories. In my performance appraisals, my supervisors often noted my "rapport-building ability." I developed the skills to make people feel comfortable, to somehow know what they needed to hear so that I could gain their trust. In essence, I was able to pick out what's important to people and use it against them—so they, in turn, would tell me what I needed to know, and I could put them in jail.

This "talent" was also helpful in learning to develop and cultivate what police call "human sources," also known as informants. Human sources are people who provide information in exchange for the following: money (typically), avoidance of a charge or reduction in the severity of whatever criminal charges have been laid against them. Working with human sources presented an interesting relationship challenge and constant negotiation. I wanted as much information as possible while giving up as little as possible in return. The source likewise wanted to give up as little information as possible while exiting whatever mess he or she was in.

Human sources are invaluable because they are often in the thick of criminal activity and know things that you couldn't possibly guess from the outside. Cultivating human sources is an exercise in using people. This mindset is hard to get out of, and you begin to see people differently. I would describe it as not seeing people at all, or as seeing what good they are to you. Many police officers—even the most productive or "good" police officers—learn how to manipulate and use people. This ability may serve us well in our jobs, but not in "real life." For me even to acknowledge this about myself took a long time, and I didn't even do as much work with sources as many do. Even now, I wonder sometimes if I am befriending someone because I want to or because I can. I know what they need to hear to be comfortable.

Back then, I was in denial, and a distance began to grow between me and my friends and family. My fiancé, Jerry, could clearly see the change in me. I was convinced they didn't understand what "real" life was like. There are bad people everywhere, I knew, and I began to resent my friends' and family's naïveté. My reality had become distorted, but instead of recognizing this, I became annoyed with them.

Gradually my closest friends and confidants were fellow police officers—the only ones who could possibly have any idea what I was going through. Having *only* other police officers as friends can be very comfortable, but it has the potential to become dysfunctional. All I did was talk about work, and most times it wasn't about the positive moments on the job. My days and nights were filled with negativity—complaining incessantly about the boss, the organization or the dirt bags. It was so easy to fall into the same mental and emotional place as everyone else. In fact, if you don't participate, you're not part of the group. Throw alcohol into the mix and it's a recipe for destruction.

Ironically, the more I tried to understand life and people, the more I didn't get it at all. One day I went to a crime scene where a man had fatally stabbed his roommate—who happened to be his brother. This was the scenario: three men in a townhouse, one having a shower and the two brothers watching television. When the man came out of the shower, he witnessed the stabbing, ran to the balcony and jumped to the ground to safety. From a neighbour's house he called 911.

I arrived on the scene with another RCMP officer to find the younger brother standing behind the sliding balcony doors in plain view, looking out at us. He wasn't co-operating with our requests to come outside, and he still had the knife in his hand. I was urging the man who had escaped to try to talk the brother into coming out, when suddenly he took the knife and plunged it into his own abdomen.

The other officer and I kicked in the door with our guns drawn. I glanced down to the basement and there was a body. All I could see were the legs sticking out and white socks covered in blood. So much blood. Bright red streaks were smeared along the walls because the victim had made his way downstairs. The carpet on the stairs was saturated, and I will never forget that metallic smell of death. We went up the stairs and located the suspect, who was lying on the floor. I kicked the knife out of his hand, and the other member handcuffed him. He was screaming that he wanted to die. We later learned that the fight had broken out because the older brother had a history of teasing and taunting the younger brother, and the younger one had just snapped. He killed his own brother in a fit of rage, stabbing him three times with a steak knife.

The twisted side of human nature was impacting me, but so was chance. Something about traffic accidents makes them hard to take. The human body is no match for cut metal and steel. An accident represents a different kind of violence.

I was riding around with Sue one night when a call came over the radio advising us of a collision on the highway. On the Trans-Canada Highway, accidents are fairly common, and most times they are serious. There are two lanes of travel in each direction with a ditch running down the middle. The posted speed limit is 110 kilometres per hour.

On this winter night, a fierce wind was blowing and snow was falling, limiting visibility even more. A nasty Alberta blizzard was brewing and causing havoc for everyone. Getting to the scene was a difficult task in itself. I was glad I wasn't driving, although being in the passenger seat wasn't much better. I'm pretty sure I left my nail impressions in the dark blue vinyl dash of the cruiser.

I wasn't on duty at the time. My civilian clothes kept me confined to the police car, where I sat taking witness statements. Sue had been outside dealing with the metal and human carnage but suddenly opened the driver's side door and sat down. She told me that the STARS helicopter could not land on the highway because of the weather. The driver of the van had been seriously injured, and the EMTs (Emergency Medical Technicians) didn't know how they were going to get the woman to the hospital. Her only chance for survival was to reach it, so she could be airlifted to Calgary. But both EMTs needed to be in the back of the ambulance with the woman, who would otherwise probably not survive the trip. They wanted *me* to drive the ambulance to the hospital.

One minute later I was staring at the dash of the ambulance.

The EMT flicked on the siren as I adjusted the seat several inches closer to the steering wheel and all the way to the top of the height adjustment. A glance at my surroundings revealed the shifter. I stepped on the brake, then placed that box-on-wheels in drive.

The road conditions had deteriorated since we arrived at the scene. It was still snowing and blowing, effectively glazing the pavement with black ice. I knew I had to hurry—a life hung in the balance—but if I went into the ditch, the woman would die for sure.

I could see, but I could also feel the relentless wind slamming against the massive body of the ambulance and causing it to slip and slide. I finally reached the curve to the exit on the highway that would take us back into town. The siren was blaring, and I could hear the voices of the EMTs—by turns calm and frantic—in the back of the unit. I picked up a little speed as I hit the main street of Brooks. The wind was still blowing, but I truly believed that the worst of the drive was over. Down the street I could see the hospital, where staff must have heard the siren, because now the steel bay door was rolling upward and inviting me in.

As I drove in to the bay, several hospital staff members rushed out the door and into the bay. The siren was still blaring, the sound amplified in that small space. Finally someone came to *my* rescue and flicked the switch to the off position. It took a minute or two to peel my stiff fingers off the steering wheel. I walked into the hospital, where the pilots of the STARS helicopter were already waiting for the woman to be stabilized. She had made it alive.

One of the EMTs came out into the hallway and told me that he was heading back to the scene of the accident. I asked him if I could go with him—this time he could drive.

He readjusted the seat controls, and we began our journey back to the highway. We turned onto the highway and as we attempted to straighten out, the ambulance hit a patch of ice and went into the ditch. Waiting for a tow truck was not an option. We abandoned the ambulance and ran down the highway to the scene of the accident. There were more injuries to tend to and the investigation of the collision was far from over.

It would be a long night.

In another accident, this time on a rural road, a young male, just seventeen years old, had rolled the truck he was driving. He had been thrown out the back window and was pinned under the truck. Two friends with him had escaped injury and managed to free him from underneath the truck, then walked several kilometres to a farmhouse, where the homeowners called for help.

When I arrived, the young man was on his back on the grass, dead. He was taken to the hospital by ambulance, and that was unusual: the ambulance isn't supposed to transport a person unless there's a chance that they can be saved.

I took a statement from his two friends at the hospital. They had been on the dirt road when the driver swerved to avoid a cow and the truck flipped. In other words, he was driving too fast and lost control. Because he was just a teenager, I was going to have to find out where his parents lived and have someone, a police officer, notify his next of kin. I sent a message to the appropriate police agency and received a phone call from the boy's father shortly after. The family was coming.

After they arrived, I escorted the father, the stepmother and the sister down to the basement where the morgue was located. A nurse came with us and brought the body out of the cooler so the father could identify his son. I stood off to the side. I wanted to give them a respectable amount of space. I remember the nurse saying, "You can touch him if you want to." I thought it was such an odd thing to say, and I actually thought, Why would you want to touch him? It's just a shell.

The nurse left to give them some time with their son's body and came over and asked me if I was okay. I told her I was fine and thought, Why are you asking me if I'm okay? It has nothing to do with me. I had never lost a loved one; I had no idea what they were going through . . . and it was probably a good thing. The boy's parents were divorced, which meant I would have to do the same thing all over again with the mother and stepfather. This was one of those times when I went "somewhere else" in my mind—when I couldn't relate and didn't want to relate. All I wanted was to get to the next call.

Notifying a victim's next of kin is one of the most difficult duties for a police officer. So many times I've had to tell a parent, son, daughter, wife, husband or other relative that they will never see their loved one again. What words of comfort would lessen the pain when delivering this kind of devastating news? I had no idea, so I didn't even try. My job, after all, was to deliver the news, not to worry about whether that news was taken well or not. My spiel was very structured. *Are you so and so? Do you have a daughter named (blank)? Please have a seat, for I have something to tell you. Your daughter (blank) has been killed in a car accident. Her vehicle was stopped on the highway and she was helping another motorist when another vehicle hit hers from behind. She's at the hospital, but please understand me, ma'am, your daughter is dead. Is there someone I can call to help you deal with what I've told you? Do you have any questions? If you do have questions later on, I'll leave my card on the table.*

I could not and would not allow myself to imagine being in their shoes—their pain.

I remember going to one woman's house in the middle of the night after her husband had been killed earlier in the evening. This marked the first time I had ever done a next-of-kin notification. I was told it's always best to go with another officer. In this situation, her husband had gone to a bachelor party for one of his friends. They had decided to fire up the dirt bikes and go for a rip around the field in the pitch dark—without headlights. Two bikes collided head-on at a high rate of speed, and one person was killed instantly. At the scene I remember shining my flashlight on the dirt bike and seeing bone and flesh stuck on the handlebars. The motorbikes themselves were nothing but bent and contorted metal.

My trainer and I drove over to the victim's residence. We walked up to the door and rang the doorbell. I can still see the wife's eyes as she looked through that half-moon window at the top of the door and flicked on the outside light. Having the police come to your door in the middle of the night is never a good sign. Luckily, she managed to unlock the door before she fainted. We helped her to a chair. I don't remember how many children she had, but it doesn't really matter. She was young, around my age at the time, and now she was a widow.

My trainer delivered the devastating news, and we stayed there until one of her family members arrived. It was difficult and awkward, and quite frankly I couldn't wait to leave. For me, once I was able to get to that front door, it was over. It was sad, and I didn't want to be sad. Police work is not supposed to be sad; it's supposed to be exciting and even frustrating, but not sad. While I was whipping around the driving course and shooting the M16 in training, I had never imagined a moment like this. Even going through the motions of delivering this kind of news in training could never compare to looking someone in the eye and experiencing the weight of that exchange. Knowing you initiated a chain of events that would change somebody's life in the worst kind of way is a heavy load to carry.

If I had *felt* everything that happened during my RCMP career, I would be sitting in the corner sucking my thumb with drool hanging off my chin. One of the most difficult scenes I ever went to was the death of a four-year-old boy. He had been feeling ill the day before and died in the middle of the night. The mother was inconsolable, and as I was unsuccessfully trying to calm her down, she went outside and stood on the curb looking up and down the street. It occurred to me what she was doing. She was waiting for a car to come by so she could step out in front of it and end her pain. I saw a car coming and grabbed her by the back of her shirt and pulled her toward me. It was so much easier to be angry with her for being unable to cope than it was to feel once again that the world made no sense.

"Everything happens for a reason." Easy for some to say. I don't want to close my eyes and see the dark blue sheets with rocket ships and stars on his bed or that small brown stain on his pillow. Anger I can deal with; sadness is on the other side of the emotional spectrum, and if I go there after seeing all that I have seen, who's to say that I will ever come back?

———————

I spent so much time at work that I really felt as though I had my finger on the pulse of the town. Once, I had just started a dayshift, when a number of break and enters were reported. I attended the scene of a few of them, and I had a good idea who was responsible. The young fellow I had in mind had just gotten out of jail, and I knew he was in town. He was well-known to all the members, and he wasn't the brightest criminal. I think he liked being caught, he liked the attention and, nine times out of ten, he would confess—because he just wanted to talk.

After attending the last reported B-and-E, I went to a house where I had executed a search warrant not long before. I didn't know if the guy who lived in the house was even associated with my suspect, but I just had a feeling, so I went with it. I walked up to the house, not calling for backup because I really had no reason to suspect that he would be there. I knocked on the door, expecting no answer because it was very early in the morning. To my surprise, the door opened, and to my even bigger surprise, the one who opened the door was my suspect.

I blurted out, "You're under arrest! Don't even think about it." He had the look in his eyes that said he was going to run. I asked him to come outside and get into the police car. He grabbed a black backpack and came outside. I explained that for our mutual safety I had to look in his bag to make sure there were no weapons. He consented, and when I opened the bag I found several watches still in their cases, some cash and assorted other goods.

I had spoken to the owner of the store that had been broken into earlier, so I knew there were watches missing. I told the suspect that he was under arrest and placed him in the back seat of the police car to transport him back to the detachment. It was obvious that he was under the influence of drugs. He was agitated and jumpy, which was unlike him. I had caught him off guard by showing up on his doorstep, and it had worked to my advantage up to this point. After a few minutes in the cruiser, however, I think he finally realized what was going on, and he became increasingly bad tempered. I got on the radio and called ahead to the detachment to advise the other members I was heading into the prisoner bay and that my prisoner was in a foul mood. My sergeant was the only other member there at the time. He, too, had dealt with this suspect before. At the detachment, I asked the suspect to get out of the car and walk over to the counter to be booked into cells. That's when he started swinging. We were able to restrain him and safely put him into cells without injury to anyone.

I waited a few hours until close to the end of my shift and then put him in the interview room. Having peeked inside his backpack, I had lots of evidence, but I wanted more. He was more reluctant than usual to talk about what he had done. He was convinced that he had been "ratted out" by the other person who was with him during his little crime spree. He wouldn't talk until I explained how I had found him. I looked him straight in the eye and said, "I guessed."

He stared at me for a minute. He said he had been ready to hear that he was captured as a result of some amazing police work, and basically wanted to know that I had spent hours upon hours tracking him down. He was devastated that luck had led me to him—luck or maybe a good old-fashioned gut feeling. He was so completely disappointed that he confessed without my having to ask him a single question. This was the latest of many B-and-E's that he had done, and as a result of this conviction and his others, he ended up going to jail for almost two years. He was a likeable guy, but he couldn't help himself. I don't think he knew what else to do. Every time he was released from jail he would come back to the same town and commit B-and-E's exactly as he had done the previous times.

For whatever reason, stuff always seemed to happen when I was working—high-speed chases, pursuits of suspects on foot. The calls kept coming, with little time to take a breath in between. Many I can recall, but more I've lost along the way, which in some ways is a relief.

What I will not forget are the few occasions when my behaviour as a police officer was called into question. During my quest to pursue justice (insert superhero music here), I also became involved in a few *internal* investigations. These investigations occur when someone you have contact with in the line of duty lays a complaint against you. The first instance occurred early in my career, and it staggered me because the stakes were so high. If found guilty, I could have been left with a criminal record and lost my job.

Even during these first years in the RCMP, I was well aware of the challenges of the profession. Mine was a thankless job that involved dealing with the most negative elements of society the majority of the time. And I knew that a thin line separated perceived right and perceived wrong as I handled these cases on a day-to-day basis. A common phrase in police work is "If you haven't been in an internal investigation, you haven't been doing your job." This is a relevant topic considering the amount of negative media attention the RCMP and other police forces are getting over cases involving possible excessive force. As with everything, there is another side, but we either don't get a chance or don't bother to tell the other side.

Sue and I were working one night and could hear yelling and screaming in a residential neighbourhood. We patrolled the area and tracked down a small group of people, one male and three females, in a back alley. We drove up beside them and requested that they quiet down, given the time of night. They informed us that they had been at the male's stag party, and it was evident they were intoxicated. All we asked was that they keep it quiet, and we were going to drive off when the male decided to become belligerent.

Sue stopped the police car and we got out. The two females got the point about being quiet and tried to contain their friend, but he was too drunk to listen. He got into Sue's space and pointed his finger in her face, and she told him to back off. Then he grabbed her by the arm. I pulled my pepper spray and gave him a short dose in the eyes. We arrested him and took him back to the detachment and provided the opportunity for him to decontaminate—to wash off the spray—and then we escorted him to the drunk tank. It was all pretty routine—until a few months later when Sue and I received a notification from the Public Complaints Commission that we were under investigation for use of excessive force.

This was my first statutory investigation where the stakes were very high because of the involvement of an external body. But I had been involved in other internal investigations, none of which had amounted to much. In one case we arrested a woman who lost control after one of her children had been bitten by a dog. She was causing a scene at the hospital, which prompted a call to Dispatch by emergency department staff. We tried everything we could think of to calm her down, but she became combative. We eventually arrested her, drove her back to the detachment and placed her in a cell.

I had seen it before. Once that heavy cell door closes shut and is locked from the outside, the reality of being in jail sets in. And people want out. In that case, the woman was both screaming *and* complaining that she couldn't breathe and needed her inhaler. I suggested to her that if she was capable of screaming, she was certainly capable of breathing. Besides, I could find no inhaler in her purse. She later filed a complaint that I had not attended to her medical needs, but the internal investigation that followed slapped my wrist and simply recommended that I do a better job of documenting prisoners' personal effects. That same woman later filed another complaint (the details escape me), but it, too, was dismissed.

As Sue had to explain to me, however, the charge of excessive force was different. This complaint against us was of a criminal nature. Section 26 of the Criminal Code of Canada states, "Everyone who is authorized by law to use force is criminally responsible for any excess thereof according to the nature and quality of the act that constitutes the excess."

Wait a minute . . . I'm the one who puts the bad guys (and gals) in jail and I need to do *what?* Get a lawyer? No, no, no, this can't be right. I went through a period of denial, believing it was a misunderstanding. No such luck. Sue and I retained a lawyer and drove to Calgary to provide statements that would then be forwarded to Crown Counsel. They would determine whether or not we would be charged with assault. This was one of the lows in my career, and I took it hard. I felt betrayed by the very public that I had committed to serving.

I had already been through a lot to help protect the public, and I had given up much personally to fulfill my duties to the best of my abilities—all of that was, in an instant, washed away. I realized it meant nothing. I was angry and bitter. Looking back, I can see that I was only about a quarter of the way to the bottom I would eventually reach. I still believed in what I was doing, and I still found the job fun at times. There was no denying the excitement. It's the same excitement people feel who slow down at accident scenes. You get caught up in the craziness. Still, it was deeply unsettling to have the finger of the law pointed at me.

I knew that some police officers did use excessive force. It's venting, for the most part. The release of negative emotions and anger follows the feeling that they have no control. A switch is flipped, and the officer becomes aggressive. I do not condone it, but I do understand it. Of course the media report on those instances when officers use excessive force, and it seems that all cops are tainted as a result.

I had taken many statements by then, and it was a surreal experience to provide a statement to someone else for the purpose of defending myself. I don't know how long the Crown took to make a decision, but it felt like forever. In the end, it was determined that my actions were reasonable, given the guy laid his hands on Sue first. His actions constituted an assault, and my reaction was justified.

I was far from relieved by the outcome. The experience changed my worldview. It made me question why I was doing what I was doing. What was the point? It was a difficult time for me, and I felt like I couldn't talk about it. The expectation of the force—and also self-imposed—was to once again suck it up and move on. Stories in the media suggest that members from different police forces are taking liberties with the public and perhaps not using appropriate discretion. It's not right that some police officers use excessive force, but it's also not right that anyone can make a complaint against good and decent police officers who have dedicated their lives to making society safer. I don't know how to balance all this. What I do know is that there seems to be a lack of empathy in society right now for the police.

Several years later, when I was working in commercial crime in Edmonton, a member from my office was arrested for domestic violence, and it highlighted my own conflict with this issue. Being a woman and having dealt with people who have experienced domestic abuse, I could easily write that member off as a no-good wife beater. But how could I ignore all that I had learned about the effects of this job? Understanding the behaviour is not the same as accepting it. He would suffer the consequences of his actions, and he would either blame everyone else or take a look at himself. My purpose in sharing my story is to start a discussion about how to reach people before they make that mistake, before they do something they can't take back.

***

One person who continues to weigh on my mind is a young girl, Lynne. Patrolling Brooks one afternoon, I saw two young girls and found it odd that they weren't in school. I ran their names through Dispatch and discovered that Lynne had been reported missing—she was a runaway. I took them both back to the detachment and contacted Social Services.

Lynne, thirteen or fourteen years old at the time, had a tendency to beat up people—male or female. Her mother was a known drug dealer and user; her sister, only slightly older than Lynne, was already pregnant. In other words, the chances of her living a "normal" life were slim to non-existent. For whatever reason, I saw something different in Lynne. I always had the feeling when I was around her that she wanted something better for herself but had absolutely no idea how to get it.

I had had someone in my life who stepped into a void and took it upon herself to teach me some of the skills I needed to live a better and richer life. She was a high school basketball coach—someone who believed in me and took an interest in me when I was acting out. Lynne was convinced that I could help her, and on some level I felt I needed to step in and be that person for her, even though deep down I knew I wasn't ready. I was still young and learning how to navigate my own way through life. What could I possibly pass on to a troubled fourteen-year-old?

Lynne latched onto me. She was always seeking me out and making it clear that she needed something from me—guidance maybe, or shelter from the storm that was her home. Lynne was a tortured soul who would break down when she was in the patrol car with me. But how could I take her in? Even though I tried to keep her at a distance, she was persistent, and the more time I spent with her, the more I felt like she was a good-hearted kid who needed someone to take an interest in her so that she could become the person she was meant to be.

Lynne was removed from her home a few times as a result of physical abuse and a variety of other issues that go with the type of environment she grew up in. I don't believe she used drugs, but alcohol was a whole different story. She bounced around to several foster homes in town, successfully wearing out her welcome at each place. Although she usually started off with a good relationship with her foster parents, eventually they would end up fighting because she often neglected curfew and other rules in the home.

She repeatedly tested her foster parents until they had no choice but to fulfill her greatest fear, which was for them to give up on her and send her back to Social Services, or worse, back home. I tried to maintain a professional distance, but developed a good rapport with her social worker and became more and more involved in Lynne's life.

If I saw her on the street at night, I would take her "home," and we would sometimes spend time talking in the police car. I was trying to pass on what limited knowledge I had, and I wanted her to feel like I believed in her, because I truly did. Still, Lynne had her ups and downs and continued to get into trouble. She was impulsive and had a temper. And she wanted more from me.

I had a feeling she wanted to live with me, but even I knew how disastrous that would be for the two of us. I took her to the gym with me on my days off, or we would go play pool. She was also a talented hockey player, and she actually played on a boys' team. I had the privilege of watching her play several times.

She could have played in college, and I tried to plant that seed. It was probably a little overwhelming for her to even consider post-secondary education. A major accomplishment would have been just to finish high school. What made it hard was the small community: all the kids her age knew she was hanging around with a cop, and I suspect that's why she got into a few scuffles (even though she would never tell me).

Her mother tried to complain about me to the detachment commander; she wanted me fired for contaminating her child. My parents even considered the possibility of taking Lynne in, but I didn't want them involved in a potentially nasty situation. Lynne and her family thrived on drama, and my parents had no idea what they would be getting themselves into. She was different from her family in a lot of ways, but she was also understandably similar. I could never completely trust her, and yet for whatever reason, she retained enough innocence throughout all her harsh experiences somehow to completely trust me.

As for my superior officers, they were neither supportive nor non-supportive. Most of them thought the die was cast for Lynne, that she would never change, and that I was crazy for getting involved. A part of me agreed, and that thought would haunt me down the line.

The foster homes in town were clearly unable to deal with Lynne, and she eventually ended up in a closed custody facility in another city. She was upset that she was being forced to leave, and I don't think I ever managed to convince her the move was wise. Lynne needed a fresh start away from the group of people she was hanging out with. While she was away, she wrote letters and kept in touch with me and seemed to be doing well. I spoke to her caseworker often, and she was kind enough to keep me updated on Lynne's progress.

One afternoon, Lynne's caseworker called me and told me that the group home was planning a trip to Waterton Lakes National Park for the weekend. All the kids were allowed to bring one family member out for the last day, and Lynne had asked her to call me to see if I would come. I wasn't sure what to do, but I couldn't leave her there feeling alone. I was working night shift that weekend, but I went home, slept for a couple of hours and hit the road.

I knew it was the right thing to do, but I really didn't understand the magnitude of her request and how vulnerable she must have felt. I made it to the lodge they were staying at, and to my surprise, I was a little nervous going in. I sat with her at a table, where we had lunch and talked. Her caseworker was there, and she spoke about the progress that Lynne had made and how important it was to her that I came. It was good to see her. I was proud of the work she was doing and told her so, and she cried.

The day we spent together included playing volleyball with the other youths and their families, and then it was time to go. Leaving was hard. Lynne would always refer to me as her friend, and I would correct her by saying that we were not and could not be friends. The joke between us was that we were acquaintances, but that wasn't really the appropriate word for it either. I saw in her something that she herself could not see—something someone had once seen in me.

I moved to British Columbia before Lynne was released from her group home. She wrote me letters, and I talked to her once on the phone. I felt I needed a fresh start by physically moving and emotionally detaching myself, carrying on with my own life—and I expected she would do the same.

I met with her again when she was eighteen years old, all

grown up and doing well. She had moved to a larger centre in southern Alberta and had a job as a security guard at one of the hospitals. She had survived. Not only had she survived but she was a contributing, functioning member of society.

I didn't hear from her for a long time after that, and then one day a police officer called me at work. Lynne was in trouble. I won't go into the details, but it was serious, and she was possibly facing criminal charges in an adult court. The detective had called me because Lynne gave her my name. I'm not sure if Lynne thought I would be able to fix this, or if she just wanted me to know what happened.

I felt like I had abandoned her, betrayed her. I felt that I had let her down in a big way, especially knowing now that she had resumed the dysfunctional lifestyle she had worked so hard to escape. Over the years I had considered contacting her or getting a message to her. I never did. Looking back, I am disappointed that I failed to understand how strongly she felt about me. I walked away from her. With the way I perceived the world at the time, it was easy for me to accept that she was destined to live the life she had been dealt. I was a fool for believing anything different.

Stepping out of my past and into my present, I have paid a price for remembering Lynne and writing about her. The past few days I have been plagued by a sore jaw—the result of my unconscious tendency to grit my teeth. This hasn't happened in a while. I've also noticed that my mood has been different. I've been grumpy lately. Thirty minutes after writing about how hard it was to leave Lynne that day, I became unusually emotional, and for no apparent reason.

Of course there is a reason. I'm reliving all of these experiences I'm writing about, only this time I'm not *physically* going through the events. I am, for the first time, experiencing the *emotions*. Many police officers cope by putting the emotions we don't want to experience in a little box somewhere, so we can perform our duties. I'm in the process of spring-cleaning, and it's a big job, but necessary to create the room I need to grow.

As I was writing this book, I was stunned to receive an email from Lynne. She told me she had been trying to find me for the past twelve years before coming across the War Horse Foundation website. I was glued to the screen as I read her lengthy email about her ups and downs. She had gone back to school: three years of college to obtain her welding credentials. She had been offered a position to teach at the college she attended but turned it down to work at a higher paying job. She has not only a job, but also a *career*. She made *it*. Her family's unbroken line of drugs and dysfunction has ended with her. How amazing is that?

Lynne wanted to give me some credit for her transformation, but that wasn't right. She was the one who did all the work, made all the right decisions. Lynne's mother, Lynne's cousins—all had died of drug overdoses. She alone had survived. Yet it struck me that we can never know how much our words and actions, which we might count as little things, can influence others. The little things I did for Lynne were not so little for her.

When you are not taught the skills you need to survive and

to succeed in life, you are at a disadvantage. Success and survival cannot just materialize out of thin air—you must be taught. Lynne learned what she needed to learn from other people and took that information and applied it in a way that made sense to her. She had people who were willing to share life skills and encourage her as she navigated her own path through her traumas. She took inspiration from others and became an inspiration to others.

There was a reason Lynne felt compelled to track me down. She was getting married and wanted me to attend her wedding. I meant it when I said that I wouldn't miss it for anything. Shortly after, I received a text from her asking if I would consider doing a toast to the bride. I responded that I would be honoured.

In August 2014, I was getting ready to make the forty-five-minute drive from where I was staying to a small town near Brooks to attend Lynne's wedding when I received a text from her: "So for the reception you're seated with family as you will see on the board. But wanted to ask you to go to one of the front rows at the ceremony with family as well! They are expecting you." It made me uncomfortable, because I felt like I didn't deserve to be there among her family. I had been out of her life for more than ten years.

It wasn't my place to argue, though, so during the ceremony I sat proudly in the front row of the hall. That's where I met Lynne's surrogate parents, who helped raise her through those difficult years. I also reconnected with one of my old soccer teammates from college. She had worked in the group home where Lynne had been a resident, and she and her parents, too, had played an integral part in guiding Lynne through the ups and downs of everyday life.

As the ceremony was about to begin, I was informed that

Lynne had made arrangements to have me transported to the location where the wedding pictures were to be taken. I was going to be photographed with her and her family. Lynne, conveniently, hadn't mentioned that part. The pictures were taken outside, and that experience made the day beautiful in more ways than one. After fighting off swarms of mosquitoes, we returned to the hall for supper.

Once the meal was over, people were called upon to deliver their toasts. The emcee made a comment about Superman and then, to my surprise, he said my name and introduced me as Lynne's "Superman."

I delivered my speech with a sense of pride that would normally be reserved for my own children. And when the music started and it was time for me to take my leave, Lynne said something to me that stopped me in my tracks. I made sure I looked her in her eyes when I responded, because it meant as much to me to say the words as it did to her. It's true that we were never friends . . . we are indeed family.

———

Lynne's story raises the question: Do people ever change? I was of the opinion that they don't, which caused me to question my own "transformation" over the past few years. I still believe that people are who they are, but I'm willing to consider that our experiences and choices can lead us closer or farther away from who we were meant to be. Initially, my own choices drew me farther and farther away from my true self, and only now do I feel like I'm on my way home again.

———

When I think about the lighter side of police work, I invariably recall that first posting in Brooks. Like the time a cow chased me on the Trans-Canada Highway, with me trying to defend myself with a shovel while thinking, Wait a minute. I'm a Mountie. I shouldn't have to *do* this! Or the time I followed tracks in the snow to capture a dimwitted thief who had stolen a snow blower—"We need that back," I told him. Or the time Sue and I chanced across an abandoned vehicle and after running the plates, discovered that the name of the registered owner sounded like "Wild Thing." I broke into the song that the British band the Troggs made famous in 1966. Sue and I were laughing so hard we could not talk to the dispatcher.

Another time we were pursuing a break and enter artist, and Sue, in the driver's seat, barked out a command: "Go get him!" As if I were her canine. I wanted to run this guy down, and she, the veteran, was content to stay in the car and drive to the alleyway where she knew he would emerge. And so he did. I would do the same later in my career. Veteran savvy, rookie adrenaline.

One time outside a bar during my first year at Brooks, I was speaking with a patron who was intoxicated, but not *too* intoxicated. "If you can make me laugh, I'll let you go," I told him. He did make me laugh, and I did let him go.

Later on in my career in the RCMP, it seemed there was less and less to laugh at as the heaviness of police work chipped away at my sense of humour. When I did laugh, it was usually at the expense of someone—maybe a knucklehead bad guy. And soon enough, black humour was all I had left.

One time when I was working in commercial crime, near the end of my career in the RCMP, I dealt with the case of a woman who had faked an illness to receive benefits, and she was caught. I called her at her new residence in Newfoundland to tell her she would be charged, and I tried to help her by giving her a list of lawyers to call. But this woman was fifty-two years old, she suffered from depression and she was looking at paying back more than $30,000. Just days after I called to tell her that she was being charged for fraud, I was notified by the local police that she had committed suicide. I felt that the system had failed her. In this case, I can honestly say that I did the best I could for her. I knew she was struggling, and I took the time to go above and beyond what I would have done earlier in my career. Her death made me sad. And that was progress. But the response of some of my colleagues was to engage in some of that black humour. They had similar cases they wanted to be done with, and they now offered those files to me, hoping for the same "results." It was tempting to laugh along with them, but it actually felt better to be sad.

My two years in Brooks were a wild mix of light and darkness. One minute, flying by the seat of my pants, the next, doubled over with laughter, and the next, facing situations that would change me forever.

CHAPTER FIVE

Crossing a Bridge

I was on duty at my second posting in Prince George, British Columbia, when I encountered a vehicle that seemed to be abandoned at the entrance to the Cameron Street Bridge—in those days an old single-lane affair, with traffic lights at either end. The bridge, more than 200 metres long, spanned the Nechako River. It was near midnight when I exited my vehicle, thinking the driver of the vehicle probably needed a tow truck or other assistance. I had exited my police car when two men stepped out from behind the truck, one of whom I recognized immediately. I had dealt with him before—and when I have cause to "deal" with someone, it's usually not a good thing. Because their vehicle appeared to be stalled, I hadn't advised Dispatch that I had stopped or that I would be out of my car for any reason. I was alone, and no one knew where I was.

From the moment we all laid eyes on one another, time seemed to slow down. I think of a police video I once watched on U.S. television—a crime re-enactment. A highway patrolman pulls over a vehicle on a main highway. There are three young men in the vehicle, and he requests that they open the trunk because he suspects that they are trafficking in narcotics. The young men obey, but then they attack him, eventually getting the upper hand and wrestling him to the ground. What happens next is every police officer's worst nightmare; they take his gun away and shoot him, leaving him for dead in the ditch on the side of the road.

Then the video is played back, and the narrator points out the moment when the two men make eye contact with each other. There are no words exchanged, no head nods. In fact, the video has to be played back in slow motion for the viewer to notice that critical moment of eye contact: a brief and silent interaction that sets in motion a chain of events that ends an officer's life.

In my real-life scenario, I, too, watched in what felt like slow motion as the two men made eye contact with each other. I knew they were going to come for me. And they did. They started around the police car, the one I recognized on my right and the other on my left. It was happening so incredibly slow, and yet I was not reacting—not even drawing my gun. All I did in that critical moment was to think, Please not in the river. I don't want to be cold when I die.

They were only steps away when, out of nowhere, a police car came around the curve. The two men took off running across the bridge. I didn't give chase. I don't remember even noticing which direction they were headed. All I could say to the other member was, "Those two guys were going to jump me." Nothing more. We searched the vehicle to try to find out what I had walked in on and found nothing. Now I was angry—beyond angry, because it had all been for nothing. But I dealt with having the vehicle towed, and then it was on to the next call.

A few months later, I responded to a call—about a male who appeared to have overdosed on drugs. The house was located in an area of town often referred to as "The Hood"—pocked with drug houses and criminal activity. I entered and walked down the stairs to the basement. There was no furniture at all, but I could see a body. On the cold, hard concrete floor was an old, filthy blue mattress and atop it someone I recognized immediately. The guy from the bridge. He was lying on his back, soaked in his own urine and feces—dead from a drug overdose.

In that moment I did not find the peace I had expected and so deeply needed. The "rule" of not speaking ill of the dead was *not* honoured in this case. I had some things I needed to say before others arrived on the scene, and some of it I did. The ambulance arrived at the house, and the body was eventually transported to the morgue.

It was over. I had won. In the epic battle of good versus evil, good had triumphed. So, then, why was I still so angry? I convinced myself I was upset because, quite frankly, his death was too easy; he didn't suffer enough. Yes, that was it. If he had suffered more, I would have had my peace. How dare he have such an easy death? All he did was die in his sleep. Coward. That wave of peace that should have washed over me and allowed me to feel good again? It never came. I felt shunned by something I couldn't quite explain. I didn't believe in any sort of God or higher being at that point. I felt as though a sense of peacefulness was unjustly being kept from me—and I resented it. There would be no cleansing on this day, nor would there be any day soon.

Over the next few months, I allowed myself to be consumed by darkness and to be ruled by anger and hatred. And I passed it on wherever I went. After I responded to complaints in those days, people did not walk away from me with a sense of being understood or any hint of compassion from me. I left those people worse off than they were before our encounter. Everyone was now the enemy.

I now realize how utterly insane those thoughts were. That man died on a filthy old mattress, and he died *alone*. He probably used drugs to numb out his own pain. How overwhelmed he must have felt. As uncomfortable as it makes me feel, I see the similarities between us now more than I see the differences. Though, lest I be accused of becoming a bleeding heart, I firmly believe that the world is a better place without him in it.

Several years later, when I told my husband about my experience on the bridge, he asked me, "What was his facial expression when he was coming at you? Was he angry?" I told him I remembered clear as day being on that bridge. The man looked to his right and made eye contact with his buddy and then looked at me. He wasn't angry or crazy looking, just the opposite. He was completely calm, with no facial expression at all—it was all business. All my husband could say was, "Oh."

The lack of emotion in that man on the bridge spoke volumes. I was angry about it for a really long time, but I was more furious with myself than I was at anyone else. I'd been in fights before and similar situations. Why didn't I move? Why didn't I try to defend myself? How could I just stand there and give up without a fight? What was that? *Who* was that? Because it sure wasn't me—or was it? No gun drawn, no pepper spray, no taking a couple of steps back to create space, no emergency call on the radio?

Without my realizing it, one part of me had begun to hold another other part of me in contempt. I could no longer be trusted.

***

Not long after the incident on the bridge, a call came about a man on another bridge—the John Hart Bridge leading to the highway that runs north from Prince George. The man had tied a sheet around his neck and said that he was going to jump off the bridge and hang himself. It was early spring and large chunks of ice were flowing down the Nechako River. He, too, was a First Nations man, well-known to police. When I heard the call come over the radio, I rolled my eyes and thought, Well, if you're going to jump, then jump, because I have lots of other things that I need to do today. It occurred to me at this point that his death would help me wrap up one of my files, because the guy on the bridge was the prime suspect.

At the scene, I briefly stood on the bridge. I could see a beer in his hand. He announced that as soon as he finished it, he would jump. My next thought was, How much beer does he have left? The negotiator soon arrived, and I took a position with some other members on the shore below the bridge. The underwater recovery team had been called out and was waiting there as well. The man must have finished up his beer, because the next thing I saw was him falling from the bridge. When he reached the end of the sheet that was tied around his neck, the sheet tore, and he plummeted toward the icy water below. He landed in a seated position on a piece of ice jammed up against one of the pillars of the bridge. From my vantage, it appeared that he then began rocking back and forth to gain enough momentum to tip himself into the water. We were advised later, at the hospital, that the landing had broken his back, so it must have taken excruciatingly painful effort on his part to finish what he had started. As this was happening, one of the members on the shore—a man with close to twenty years' service—started to run toward the water, and it took several of us to hold him back. Along with the other members, I was livid that the officer would put himself and the rest of us in jeopardy for the sake of some dirt bag. What was he thinking?

The underwater recovery team went into the river and retrieved the body. One of the members who was on the shore asked me if I had ever seen the process that medical staff go through in an effort to revive someone in that condition. I said that I had not, so off to the hospital we went. I vividly remember being in the hospital room. The doctor and nurses were working vigorously to save this person, though he had been under water a long time. I felt a surge of anger. The time and money being put into this resuscitation effort was, to my mind, outrageous. I was so angry that I looked right at the dead man's face. I've always tried to avoid looking at the eyes of the dead because they will return to haunt me in the middle of the night. His eyes were wide open and completely blank. He was gone, and he wasn't coming back.

I have had a lot of time in the intervening years to think about those eyes, and yes, they have visited me in the night. I now believe that the reason the scene has stayed with me is that I knew his eyes were a reflection of my own at the time, dark and empty. I had become who I thought I needed to be in order to survive my new reality. As for the RCMP officer who wanted to risk his own life to save another, he hadn't been thinking at all. He was the only one there that night who was *feeling*.

––––––––––

A question that I continue to ponder is: How does one do this work and maintain some level of compassion? Is it possible to work as a police officer and maintain a sense of balance . . . a sense of self? If you let compassion rule you, especially in a moment of crisis or threat, then your own life will be in danger. And yet, if you eliminate compassion from the equation, hardness sets in. It sets, like cement, in your bones. It's like trying to draw a picture with your left hand while doing a math problem with your right. The two can't be completed simultaneously. You must do them one at a time. And more often than not, by the time I was finished dealing with a crisis, I had little time, energy or inspiration to keep compassion at the forefront of my everyday dealings with people.

Police officers and other first responders will often risk their lives to save others (including animals) who are in danger or under threat. It is a completely different scenario than having one's own life threatened. I know that when that primal response of fight or flight is triggered, there is no choice. Choice is replaced by instinct and reaction.

Once you see for yourself what humans are capable of, you can never go back. You step through the door of innocence and you hear it slam shut behind you.

If you don't take the time to understand and, in some respects, grieve that loss of innocence, then it builds as resentment and a

sense of betrayal. I remember going back to one of my instructors at college and asking him, "Why didn't you tell me it was
going to be like this?" His answer: "Because you wouldn't have
believed me."

Who on earth would knowingly sign up for this job—for
what it really is? Most people join the police for the excitement
of high-speed pursuits, chasing bad guys and/or helping people.
Nobody tells you about the psychological impact the job will
have on you. They don't tell you that you will see things that
will haunt you in your sleep: children killed in car accidents or
sexually assaulted or physically brutalized—usually by a family
member. They don't tell you that you will in all likelihood lose
faith in humanity. And that no matter how hard you work, the
calls will just keep coming—there is no end. Some calls may turn
into great stories about the stupid things that people do, and you
will laugh, but never for long.

———

The close call on one bridge, the suicide on another—they were
significant moments in my life when home was Prince George,
British Columbia. If my first posting in Brooks, Alberta, was
about drugs and alcohol, my second posting in Prince George
was the same, but heavily layered with despair, struggle and
suffering.

I had landed in Prince George by a circuitous route. After
more than two years in Brooks, it came time to make some
decisions. I contacted staffing—the unit responsible for all
employee transfers—and requested that I be transferred to
Grande Prairie, closer to where my fiancé, Jerry, then worked.

The long-distance relationship between us was well into its third year. In response to my request, I received notification that I was already "suitably posted."

Staffing advised me they would be willing to entertain a transfer in another three to five years. Sue had transferred out by then. She had grounded me, and especially with her gone, living and breathing my job began to take a toll. Attempting to maintain a long-distance relationship was exhausting. I knew I had to make a change if I wanted to keep my relationship with my fiancé, so I decided to take a one-year LWOP—a leave without pay.

I applied for a job as a claims adjuster with the Insurance Corporation of British Columbia (the same organization that employed my fiancé) and got one in Prince George. Though he worked for a different department and though we were not yet married, they transferred Jerry to Prince George within weeks of my starting at my new job. That's what a compassionate employer does. How different that was from what I was used to.

I had a year to make the decision about whether or not I would return to the RCMP. On the one hand, the corporation was the best workplace I had ever known; on the other, I soon knew this claims adjuster gig wasn't for me. I was like a race-car driver who had quit his job to become a driver examiner for novices and seniors. ICBC offered me a position in their Special Investigation Unit in the Lower Mainland, but this wasn't ideal either. Would my fiancé be transferred as well? Would we be able to afford to live in Vancouver?

An incident had occurred during that past year that weighed heavily on my mind and on my decision. I had had a run-in with the local outlaw motorcycle gang, affiliated with the Hells Angels, in Prince George. After interviewing the president of this local gang, I denied an insurance claim of a stolen vehicle, and one of the associates started to harass me at work. I was filled with frustration over the injustice. I felt powerless in this situation, and missed the authority I had once had to deal with these types of people. I realized the only way I could effectively fight for justice was to return to the RCMP.

Then an ICBC employee whose husband was an RCMP member in Prince George offered to initiate a conversation with the local detachment and inquire if they would take me on. Shortly after, I received a call from a member at the detachment stating they would gladly take me on. (They don't exactly have members beating down the door to work in Prince George, a rough community with more than its fair share of issues.) My return came at a time when the RCMP was running short on members and spots were open in most detachments.

My fourteen-month experience at ICBC had been a positive one, and I met some very good people there. If I hadn't worked there, I probably never would have taken the time to get to know people outside the RCMP. I knew it was going to be an uphill battle going back to the RCMP; when you leave the force for whatever reason and go back, it's usually not looked on well by the other members. Individual circumstances are not taken into consideration. I was sure I would be lumped in with the useless who "can't take it" or "can't do the job." I would be seen as an outsider—even though I had never stopped being a member.

Before making my final decision to go back to the RCMP, I went out on a ride-along with two members in Prince George.

They were on C Watch—one of four watches at the detachment (A, B, C and D) that rotated on twelve-hour shifts. At the time, my fiancé was also working shift work, and ideally we wanted to arrange it so we had our days off together. It so happened that the members I knew on C Watch were on the rotation that would allow me to take those days off—perfect. The transition would also be easier because I would know a few people.

After the ride-along, I expressed my desire to go to C Watch and was told that although C Watch was short, A Watch was shorter. I would be assigned to A Watch. I explained the situation to the member in charge of staffing at the detachment and was told to take it or leave it. The conversation began in my head: What have I done?

Early in the year 2000, I accepted the position on A Watch, where I ran up against a small clique of members. My life became a lot more difficult than it needed to be. Those in the group were mostly male, with one token female, who was mocked by her trusted comrades when she wasn't around. It appeared to me they had no real loyalty to one another but shared a willingness to torment others.

One of these members, in particular, was known to be anti-female—despite being married to a female member. A high-ranking officer told me he knew about this particular member and about his negative attitude toward female members, but he said his response to the problem was "What are ya gonna do?" For the most part, the A Watch clique did their best to ostracize me and talk negatively behind my back. They wouldn't offer any assistance when I went to a call, and eventually I did the same. Ultimately, we parted ways.

I had a good relationship with several members of the watch, and I would like to say I was happy with that—but in truth it was a difficult time. Looking back, I believe what set me apart was my time spent in "normal" society. Through my time at ICBC, I had been given a taste of the outside world, and I liked it. I wasn't like the other members anymore, and I was okay with that, but unfortunately it didn't make my work any easier.

My saving grace was a capable and competent supervisor who took the time to assess members as individuals. The night he rode with me in a police car, I ended up in a foot chase downtown and caught the guy and dragged him back to the vehicle. After that night, I felt confident that he would judge me based on my abilities and competence on the job. And to his credit, that is exactly how it played out. Looking back, I have to admit: I made mistakes in dealing with the A Watch clique, and I'm not particularly proud of myself in some respects. I regret not being the bigger person and at least offering my assistance and showing up on some calls—regardless of my reception. I didn't always do the right thing, and I regret that.

Life on A Watch was certainly eventful. Soon after I started, I volunteered to be on the Team Policing Unit. Another member and I were responsible for the downtown core area and would often patrol on bicycles and on foot. We responded to any calls in the downtown area, including a residential area used by sex-trade workers.

The offences were violent in nature, as can be expected where there's a high degree of drug and alcohol use. My partner was a good and easygoing guy. Prince George was his first posting, but his father was in the RCMP, so he was familiar with life according to the force. We worked well together, and I was always comfortable being around him. He made life bearable, and for that I am grateful.

Being on Team Policing effectively threw me back into the thick of things. So much happened in such a brief period of time. I saw things there that I never could have imagined. Five- and six-year-olds were walking around in the middle of the night looking for their parents, who were in bars. There were bodies on the street, passed out. There were people in alleys or in the bushes sniffing chemicals from spray cans or drinking cheap wine. Prince George was a different world, an alternate reality.

———

Then there was my time with the so-called Green Team—investigating marijuana grow operations. I was the first female member to participate, and I had anticipated there would be some resistance. I was right. Other members of my team would do things like not share Crime Stoppers tips with me. Or when we conducted a search of a residence, they would set up the entry plan and not have me go into the house, but rather wait back on the perimeter. I saw that as sabotage of a subtle kind.

Then there was the more blatant kind. Almost every grow op we raided had dogs on the property—pit bulls, Dobermans, Rottweilers. We all had a drawer in a designated filing cabinet at the office. Someone stuck labels on the front: the top one was "Dog Master" and the next one down was "Dog Trainer" and so on. My drawer, of course, was on the bottom, and the label stuck to the front was "Dog Bait." This would have been funny had we all been friends or good colleagues, but we weren't.

One time we were executing a warrant on a house with a grow operation; the owners were known to be violent and there was a high probability of weapons on-site. In these situations, we would request that the emergency response team do the entry and our team would follow. I was sitting in the ERT locker room with a bunch of semi-automatic gun-toting hot shots. The entry plan had been developed, and everyone had a role to play. When we were preparing to leave, one of the guys looked at me and gave a little war cry: "Let's go, boys!" I couldn't help but smile. But then, as I was standing at the door, a fellow from the ERT team walked by and said, "Look out, little girl, the boys need to go take care of business."

I was no stranger to being around "the boys." I had received a scholarship to play on the men's soccer team in college, and I had played on several other men's teams. I have no problem holding my own both physically and verbally with members of the opposite sex. This was the first time I've ever really felt a division between men and women at work. I didn't like it.

Nevertheless, our team put together more warrants than any previous team, and we busted several grow ops during the few months we participated on the unit. It was fun skulking around in the middle of the night gathering information. Sometimes we would go into work at three or four o'clock in the morning. The hours were crazy, but it was worth it. All in all, it was a good experience, and I earned a written letter of acknowledgment from the sergeant in charge of the drug section for the work I did. In his commendation, he noted that I wrote more warrants and seized more marijuana plants than any other member on the team, and he noted the obstacles I had to endure in working with a group of "strong personalities."

Black leather jacket. Tight jeans. Zipped-up boots to the knees. Poofy hair and lots of makeup. I was twenty-eight years old and working the midnight shift, standing on a street corner where sex-trade workers plied their trade. I was part of an RCMP sting operation, undertaken in response to complaints from citizens of the town.

When the sergeant in charge of the drug section at the Prince George detachment had asked me to pose as a street prostitute, I agreed. So a couple of days before my shift, I huddled with some of the women on my local soccer team, and they helped me choose the right garb.

In my time with the force, I only participated in these operations a few times, but I wasn't prepared for the impact the work had on me. My view of men took a beating after seeing fathers roll up to the curb with baby car seats in the back. The majority of women working street corners in Prince George were aboriginal, and most were on drugs. They didn't, as I had assumed, do sex work to pay for a drug habit; they took drugs to help them stomach the work, which they did out of desperation. They needed money to live, so they sold their only commodity: their bodies. Their souls soon followed.

I went in with little knowledge about sex-trade workers and the "industry" as a whole. But I thought, What better way than to ask these girls myself? I didn't hide who I was; I did this from inside a marked police car. Some were willing to talk, while others would rather have stuck a sharp object in their eye than be seen talking to the police. Fair enough. At first most were leery about saying anything at all, but slowly I gained their trust to the point that I could at least approach them without being sworn at or given the finger.

I had a genuine interest in their lives, and I wanted to know their stories. I was once again that sponge that I had been earlier in my career—thirsty to know more. I wanted to understand.

"Do you have a spotter?" I would ask them. A spotter is some-one—male, female, perhaps a relative, perhaps a pimp—who watches and notes what kind of car she gets into. Prostitution, and especially street prostitution, is a dangerous profession, and having a spotter is a safety precaution. Someone who can inter-vene if need be or write down a licence number.

I spent time getting to know these girls—and I call them "girls" not out of disrespect, but because to call them women cre-ates the expectation that they had the wisdom and self-esteem to change the course of their lives. Unfortunately, they had no one around to pass those virtues on to them. Although most would say they are anything but innocent, that's the word that comes to mind when I remember them.

The first time I was asked to go undercover as a sex-trade worker, it seemed a great opportunity, but also a challenge. I am a quiet and reserved individual, and to play this role would require that I tap into something that I wasn't sure I had. I wondered if I could engage in conversation with someone—a male, who would basically solicit me for sexual purposes—without giving in to the impulse to punch him in the face.

The Prostitution Unit from Vancouver came up, and I was one of three undercover operators scheduled to stand on a desig-nated street corner waiting for the "johns" to approach. One of the operators became ill, and so it was just two of us "working." The other member from Vancouver had done it a few times before, and I watched her for the first while. Wearing tight pants and with a sucker hanging out of her mouth, she stood out on the corner until she was approached. She would engage various men in conversation, but she didn't have a microphone or recording device. She would give a pre-selected signal when it was time for the cover team to race in and take the male into custody. Another member would then lead her away to the safety of the van we were sitting in.

Then it was my turn. That was a long walk, that first walk to the corner from the van. I was extremely nervous. I had taken great care in assembling my outfit, and around my waist I carried a fanny pack containing a cellphone, a condom (for show) and pepper spray. I knew that the conversation I would have with the "customer" had to cover the necessary elements to establish the offence of soliciting a prostitute in a public place. I won't reveal specifics, but I will say that this detailed discussion took me well beyond my comfort zone. Still, I turned out to be quite good at it. This was a game, and at the time, I still liked games.

A few encounters stand out in my mind. There were several occasions when the "customer" I was talking to suspected I was a police officer. One guy didn't want to say too much in case I was wired. I explained to him that time was money and that he was wasting mine. He insisted on continuing the conversation and came up with what he thought was the brilliant idea of writing down what he wanted. I was hard pressed to hold back a chuckle, but I accepted his idea. He grabbed a small piece of paper and wrote down "Lay $50." I looked at it and nodded, and he placed it in his glove box. Of course, shortly thereafter it was seized as evidence by the take-down team. We all had a good laugh about that one.

One john initiated a conversation and pulled out a picture of his pet moose. He seemed harmless enough, until he asked if he could "touch them." I said, "Touch what?" and he said, "Your breasts, to prove that you're not a cop." As I took an involuntary step backwards, I countered with, "Touching ain't free." I'm not sure what I would have done had he tried to touch me, but I'm quite certain my cover would have been blown and the take-down team would have had to enter the picture to prevent him from sustaining any injuries. Those tiny little hairs on the back of my neck pricked up, and for a moment it wasn't a game anymore.

Through this work, I caught a glimpse of what a sex-trade worker's life is really like. Once, I was standing on the corner, not talking to anyone, when a car drove by. The occupants, kids in their late teens or early twenties, called me names and threw containers of hot sauce, the kind from fast-food restaurants. Fortunately, their aim was as low as their IQ.

Another time a truck pulled over to the curb, and I walked over to the driver's side window. The driver just pointed to the passenger. The male in the passenger's seat piped up and said, "I can't even see what the bitch looks like. Tell her to get her fuckin' ass over here." As I counted down slowly from ten to get a handle on my anger at being spoken to that way, I walked around the back of the truck to the passenger side window. We made a deal, and it was my absolute pleasure to give the signal for the cover team to move in and arrest him. This fellow, it turns out, had a criminal record—for sexual assault.

I've experienced being hated before because I'm a police officer, but it was a perspective-changing experience to feel hated because I was a woman. As I relive that experience, I can feel that surge in me as I felt it that night, and I distinctly remember looking into the eyes of the source of that hatred and reacting the only way I knew how: hate him right back, only more so. No flashing kind of emotion, this came from somewhere deep. But inside I was disturbed—disturbed that I could go there and that it felt good in some way. It was easier to feel the hate than to feel anything else.

I was asked to play the role of sex-trade worker a few more times, and during those nights I acted as the sole undercover operator. Common practice was to run a double sting and have a male undercover operator solicit female sex-trade workers before the undercover sex-trade workers went out. This served a double purpose: it eliminated competition and made it safer for us. Pimps and other prostitutes can become confrontational when new faces appear on the street, and I had little protection against any potential threat. A cover team was watching from several vans parked a block or two away, but lots of things could happen in the minutes it would take for them to respond. Compounding the problem were johns who wanted to move to a more private location to continue the negotiation.

I was on the sidewalk once and noticed a female coming toward me. I recognized her right away as someone I'd arrested before. I also knew she had AIDS. My phone rang in my pouch; it was my supervisor, asking me if I knew the female coming down the street and what I wanted to do. I had to decide if I wanted to head back to the van, or wait and see how the situation was going to unfold. I thought it was possible she might recognize me.

I was well aware of the violence she was capable of, and I had no desire to tangle with her. She no doubt possessed some sort of weapon and was likely high on either drugs or alcohol. Best-case scenario: she would just continue on her way. Worst-case scenario: she would decide to defend her territory. It was a tense moment. By now, part of the cover team was out of the van and waiting to respond if need be. I don't know if she saw them or recognized me, but she thought better of coming any closer. Then she yelled, *repeatedly*, "Fuckin' cop!" Cover blown. We shut the operation down. Tomorrow was another day.

On one of the many occasions I had encountered this woman, I was on foot patrol downtown with my partner when we received a call that two women were fighting outside. Both suspects lived on the street and were known sex-trade workers. They had gotten into a fight all right—not with their fists, but with broken beer bottles. There was blood everywhere on the sidewalk. The woman I recognized was screaming, and when we called out her name, she turned, and we could see there was a big flap of skin hanging from her left cheek.

We all knew she had the HIV virus. The Emergency Medical Services (EMS) arrived to treat her wounds, but she was less than co-operative. Our options were to let her pass out from loss of blood, incapacitate her with pepper spray or calm her down enough that she could be attended to. After a brief discussion, the EMS team decided to grab a blanket, and as my partner and I distracted her, they rushed her, wearing masks and rubber gloves, and wrapped her in a blanket with her arms tucked inside. She was eventually transported to the hospital.

We arrested her more than once for being intoxicated in a public place, and every time we would bring her back to cells, we would almost immediately get called back by the guard because she was lying on the cell floor foaming at the mouth. She looked to be in medical distress, so we would inevitably call the ambulance, and she would be transported to the hospital. There, her condition would suddenly and dramatically improve. She was apparently able to foam at the mouth on demand.

When I tell people about these undercover experiences, they are fascinated and imagine the adventure of it all. The experiences *were* exciting, and they did challenge me to think quickly on my feet. They were also exercises in self-control. But I didn't deal with them properly, and I failed to process them, which caused them to land once again in my internal garbage Dumpster. By this time in my career, my Dumpster was on the verge of overflowing.

I remember one of my first shifts in Prince George, when I arrested a well-known street person and took him up in the elevator from the prisoner bay to the cell area. I was holding on to his arm so he wouldn't fall over, and he looked at me and slurred, "Just don't beat me." I thought it was an odd thing to say, and in my mind I said, Don't be ridiculous. These homeless men and women self-medicated with alcohol, so they were always intoxicated, and, more often than not, belligerent. Others shuffled along robotically, playing out their own deeply embedded routine.

I grew up in a place that was predominantly Caucasian, and my first posting was very diverse ethnically, but Prince George marked my first interaction with First Nations people. I came in with no preconceived notions. People are people, and I believed that everyone deserved respect until they gave me a reason not to be respectful. I understood that the men and women I saw on the streets of Prince George represent a small population of First Nations people, and it is not my intention to paint everyone with the same brush. But these were my experiences.

It was frustrating, shift after shift, to be called about the same people—homeless First Nations people with severe substance abuse issues. They were filthy, diseased and raunchy, with the unforgettable smell of urine and feces mixed with alcohol. I eventually referred to them in my mind as "vermin."

I feel relieved not to carry that burden anymore, and yet incredibly ashamed to think and write that word. It's not an easy place to go back to, but that's how I felt at the time. The people on the streets were, in my mind, not people at all. I came to view them as wastes of skin who served no purpose other than to annoy me and take up my precious time. This attitude is "understood" in most policing circles, but never really talked about. I developed a hatred toward a group of people, and it came as a result of judgment and a feeling of superiority. How could I have avoided it? Even now in hindsight, I can't offer any real solution. I viewed them—and they viewed me—as a constant threat. In this environment, we were enemies, and to have believed anything less would have been to put myself at risk.

Any race or ethnic background could have triggered that sentiment. Had all these people on the street been Latino or Asian or African, the same antipathy would have arisen. What matters here is the judgment and my perceived inability to do anything about it. I felt so helpless and useless to change the situation—one I hated. These homeless people were trapped in an unending cycle of poverty, violence and addiction, and I was trapped in my own cycle of hate and disgust, which caused me to do things and think things that I had never imagined I could. How could I behave in this way and have these thoughts and still, in my heart, believe I was a good person?

One night the detachment received a call from an employee at the needle exchange. She either remembered she hadn't locked the doors to the building or someone called and told her that the door was unlocked. Regardless, she called the detachment to request that we check the front doors of the exchange and let her know if it was secure. My partner and I drove up and noticed someone inside. It was "Ella," a native woman who lived on the streets. I don't recall how old she was, probably in her twenties, but she had diminished mental capacity. Everyone at the detachment "knew" Ella, for she was in our cells on a regular basis. The question was not *if* we were going to pick her up during the shift, but when, and how bad a shape she was going to be in. I didn't like dealing with her—not because she was particularly difficult, but because she was so dirty. She was a hard-core street person who rarely washed.

We pulled up to the building and noticed her inside. We were expecting her to be either stealing something or vandalizing the property, but instead she had a broom in her hand. She was sweeping the floor and cleaning up, pretending that she worked there.

The moment wasn't completely lost on me—for a change. I knew I was seeing something significant, something worth remembering. Watching her walk around and empty the dustpan into the garbage and then stand up straight and look "normal," I felt her sense of pride. She was taking care of something; she was being responsible, and clearly it made her feel good inside. For the first time I could remember, she was actually beaming. There was a lesson in there somewhere for all of us.

When we walked up to the front door, Ella didn't acknowledge our presence. We went in and looked around and told her that she had done a great job, but now it was time to go. Both my partner and I wanted her to leave with her pride intact. She walked out that door into the night and back into her reality.

CHAPTER SIX

Deaf to My Entreaties

W hen I left Prince George in 2002, I was not the same person as when I had arrived. I don't remember laughing or feeling any real sense of happiness. My experience there had confirmed my outlook on people, and it wasn't a positive one.

My first detachment in Brooks had opened my eyes to how some people treat each other and what the human race is capable of. Yet there was palpable excitement there. Prince George felt like a descent into disillusionment. There will always be, I told myself then, another marijuana grow operation to bust, more organized crime, more intoxicated men and women lying passed out on the sidewalk, more violence and more suffering. It seemed there was no end to the suffering. And I began to question what I was doing. What was the point? I was weary of my own despair, and weary, too, of all the little wars. I was fighting with the public (complainants were often uncooperative, suspects were both uncooperative *and* belligerent, and the public just never seemed satisfied with the service they were getting—they always wanted something more). I was in conflict with other officers on my watch. I was tired, and it felt like it was time to move on.

Jerry's job had become unstable, the health-care system in Prince George was well below average, and I was pregnant and wanted to be closer to my family. It was time, I felt, to leave, and I had all these justifications. In hindsight, I know that I was running. I've seen the same thing dozens of times with other members. We're eager to get out of the detachment we're in, with hopes of sunshine and rainbows and a fresh start somewhere else. Unfortunately, the only dynamic that changes is the location. Other than the dot on the map, it's the same shit, different pile.

I was doing my best to control my own destiny, even though that's considered taboo by most in the force. My plan was to move once I was on maternity leave, and I would then have a year in Alberta to convince staffing to put me somewhere. During my time in Prince George, I had gained valuable experience in a variety of different areas. My perspective was that it could be a win-win-win move for my family, the RCMP and me.

My departure from the Prince George detachment was quiet. I only told a few of the other members on my watch that I was leaving. My detachment commander knew, of course, but the other members didn't know, and I didn't want to bear the brunt of their reaction to my news. Their assumption would be that I couldn't handle it. In some ways they would be right, but not for the reasons they would think. I could handle myself and I could handle the job of policing. What I couldn't come to grips with was all the crap in between.

My commanding officer supported my leaving—on paper. And that was a huge boost. He knew what difficulties I would face trying to re-enter the force in Alberta and kindly wrote a letter in support of me.

Jerry and I found a house in a community outside Edmonton. There weren't many houses for sale, and we were lucky to find one in a quiet neighbourhood—a place we could potentially afford on one salary if it came to that. After moving to Alberta for several weeks of training, Jerry came back to Prince George, and, with the help of my parents, we loaded up the U-Haul and were Alberta bound.

My first priority in the new community was finding a doctor, because the baby was due soon. Most doctors were not accepting new patients, but fortunately, one doctor was willing to take on pregnant patients. Jerry and I signed up for prenatal classes, and shortly thereafter—on November 14, 2002—we became the parents of a beautiful baby girl we named Skylar.

I was glad to be back in Alberta. I like to think that I'm an independent person, but it felt good to be nearer to my family— even though they were still six hours away. And once Jerry's parents retired, they would be moving even closer. I think about how many members in the RCMP are stationed across the country and raise their families with no help from anyone.

The choice I had made to come back to Alberta—with the support of my commander but, once again, against the overall wishes of my organization —was not taken lightly, but I truly believed that all parties could be served in the end. I had valuable operational experience, and at the end of the day, the RCMP is a *national* police force. With so many vacant positions in Alberta, I decided to take my chances and trust that common sense would prevail. Despite everything I knew and had experienced about how the organization operated, for some reason I still believed it should and would work out.

I took the first few months to settle in and try to get a handle on motherhood. I knew that would be a challenge. Nurturing didn't come easily to me, and the thought of being off work for a whole year frightened me. I didn't see myself as stay-at-home-mom material. The move to Alberta proved to be the right one because it allowed my mother to play an important role in helping me through this transition. I still very much identified with being a police officer, and I was focused on salvaging that identity. With the trauma that I had been through, I was not functioning from a healthy place. Stress over the possibility of losing my identity as a police officer triggered my fear response. A few months into my maternity leave, I started the process of finding a position close to where I lived.

My initial discussions with staffing were met with resistance and suggestions that I return to B.C. with or without my family— that part would be up to me to decide. I was told that I had been misinformed and that, in fact, there weren't *any* vacancies in Alberta. My experience told me that a member in the RCMP doesn't move on his or her own accord and agenda—twice— without consequences. I had known I would have to pay a price, and I had expected to have to commute to my next detachment. But I had never anticipated that the RCMP would deny me a job unless I went back to Prince George. The organization had spent the time and money to train me, and I was good at my job; it simply didn't occur to me that they would leave me on the bench when the province was running with hundreds of vacancies. I was determined to find out for myself whether or not there were any positions available in the surrounding detachments. I am a trained investigator, so I decided to investigate.

After a few short weeks, I learned that every detachment in the surrounding area was short at least one member. In some cases, the vacancy rate was at a critical level. At the RCMP detachment in my own community, I spoke to the detachment commander, a staff sergeant who was impressed with my experience. He told me he had just spoken with staffing and put in a specific request for a female member with more than five years' experience who was also D.A.R.E. trained. (I had taken the Drug Abuse Resistance Education training and had briefly taught Grade 5 pupils in Prince George.)

Check, check and check. The added bonus was that they wouldn't even have to pay for a transfer. I was already right here. I even agreed to come back from my maternity leave early and start right away. The staff sergeant said he would contact staffing, but it looked to him like a good fit.

My next call came from a staff sergeant, this one in charge of the staffing and personnel section in K Division. He told me to stop going to the different detachments; I was not allowed to do that. (Clearly he had received a few phone calls from these detachments wanting to take me on.) He advised me that detachments don't make decisions on staffing matters and that *his* unit was in charge of placing members. I asked him if he would please put in writing that there were no positions available in the area. But of course he would not, because he *could not*. It wasn't true.

Two days later, I received another call. Suddenly they had an opening. A small detachment at Redwater, 40 kilometres from my home, had an "operational need" for my services. I was transferred as STE (Surplus to Establishment), which meant that the detachment was at full capacity and I would be an extra body. A member was currently on maternity leave and the decision had been made to fill that position—which never happens. I would have a thirty-minute commute, I would be on-call because the detachment wasn't big enough or busy enough to offer twenty-four-hour coverage, and I would be required to sign a document stating that after this posting, I would not seek another in the Edmonton area. The RCMP were fulfilling their obligation of offering a position; if I turned it down, there wouldn't be another opportunity.

Mine was a punishment posting, and in the fall of 2003, I took my punishment. All the paperwork was faxed, and I reluctantly signed in all the appropriate boxes. I wasn't happy about the position I was in, and I was being treated with much less respect than was called for, but I didn't have a choice. Obviously I *did* have a choice, but I felt powerless.

I was no stranger to starting over, and I decided I needed to make the best of it. If I could ride this out for three years or so, I would have experience at a small detachment, a medium-sized detachment, and a large detachment. I would be extremely well-rounded and in a good position to be promoted to the next level. I had had the experience of working in two busy detachments, and now, being in a smaller and less busy one, I would have the time to do the work I enjoyed. I made a plan. I would take down some grow ops, develop some informants and work my way out of this place. I could use this posting to my advantage; all I had to do was put my head down and get it done.

But a major problem at this detachment—one that can

arise anywhere—soon revealed itself. The officers were young and hardworking, but the sergeant who had been running the detachment had just been transferred to another one. The RCMP often does this when leadership issues cause, eventually, a dysfunctional detachment. When I arrived, the change was only half complete, and we waited anxiously to find out if the replacement commander would be good or bad news.

The word was that our new leader was going to be a woman, and the initial opinion was, typically and unfortunately, less than favourable. I can't say if the response is different toward women in municipal or provincial police forces, but in the RCMP that's how it was, and is.

I was always of the opinion that the majority of men were fine working with women as long as we did our job. For the most part, we don't want to be thought of as "women" anyway when we're in uniform; gender shouldn't even be part of the conversation. I always shake my head when I see an article in a newspaper and the reporter makes a point of mentioning that the RCMP officer on the scene was female. You never read, "A male police officer arrested the suspect."

In Prince George, after one of our morning briefings, our watch commander had handed out an envelope to each female member in the room. In the envelope was a survey designed to determine how female members felt they were being treated in their current law enforcement roles. An awkward moment, to say the least. He made some joke about it and sent us on our way. I remember being furious—not at my watch commander, but at those who had sent out the survey. Why couldn't they just leave us be? Why draw attention to us? Being promoted just *because*

I'm a female or getting some sort of special treatment *because* I'm a female is not the kind of "equality" I was ever looking for. I threw the unopened envelope in the garbage.

I was getting ready at home for my second or third shift at Redwater, when I grabbed the mail from my mailbox and spotted the newspaper inside. The front-page headline read something like, "Local RCMP Desperately Seeking Members." I could feel my face flushing. I was livid.

The article described how the community detachment was dangerously short on members, with no relief in sight. The staff sergeant I had previously talked to was quoted. I couldn't believe it. I drove to work, sat down at the computer and started writing up a grievance. I had never gone through the grievance process before, but I didn't care. I was up for the fight. I kept this to myself because I worried it would cause a problem with either the corporal in charge or the other members. This wasn't a case of not wanting to be in Redwater; working where I lived would simply have been much better. My placement flew in the face of good sense.

I felt betrayed. I had been around long enough to have little faith in the grievance process, but in this situation, I felt I had a chance. If I could just prove there were positions open at the RCMP detachment in my own community, I would be awarded the transfer and have an opportunity to live and work in my community. In the meantime, I would have to stay the course until either my grievance was accepted or I got a promotion.

The first step of the grievance process is to attempt informal resolution. I contacted my SRR (Staff Relations Representative), who is supposed to act on my behalf—much like a union representative. The SRR is a member of the RCMP who is elected by the members; however, this person is not separate from management, and that has been a source of controversy ever since I started my career. I had been advised many times by fellow officers that if I ever got into trouble, I was *not* to contact my SRR—an officer torn between allegiance to members and allegiance to management (with his or her own career status added into the mix). And the latter two considerations are much more important than the first. Regardless, I needed help because I'd never gone through this process, and I needed help if I was going to succeed.

The system looks good on paper: The SRR is elected by members and can be dumped by members after a term is served. But few members actually believe the system works and see no point in bringing in a new person. And it became clear in the meeting to consider my case that my SRR, a sergeant, knew the member from staffing. The meeting was hardly underway before I had a feeling it was a sham.

I was arguing that there were, in fact, positions available at my local RCMP detachment. The staffing person was unwilling to concede that, and argued that there were no positions available in Alberta, let alone my community. At the end of the meeting, nothing was resolved. Neither of us was willing to budge, and my SSR was not interested in pushing her into releasing the information—and indeed was powerless to do so. I was fuming by the end of the meeting. When there was nothing further to talk about, I left, while my representative stayed behind and had some chuckles with "the enemy." I had the distinct feeling I had been duped by the process. At this rate, I would be eligible for another transfer long before my grievance was resolved.

I soon found out that policing in a small community wasn't all fun and games. The community wanted more than just policing—they were big into *community policing*.

I hadn't signed up to be a school liaison or to put on a bike rodeo for the kiddies, or for school tours, or committees, or any of that other stuff that has absolutely nothing to do with catching bad guys. I didn't *do* community policing.

From my perspective, the worst news came when I was chosen to be the Victim Services Liaison. In Prince George, I had attended a major crimes conference, and one of the speakers was the sister of a man who had been shot while he and his wife were riding horses on their own property. As a result of some impressive police work, they managed to catch the person responsible—the victim's neighbour. The two neighbours had squabbled; one thing led to another, and finally one shot and killed the other.

The sister took the podium and spoke about how the RCMP officers on the scene could have done a better job of dealing with the victim's family. I could feel the blood rush to my cheeks as she spoke. I looked around at the table to see if anyone else was thinking what I was thinking. I made eye contact with one of the other members at my table, and yes, we were on the same page. The sister of the victim talked about how more compassion could have been shown by the members. I wanted to stand up and say, Really? Shouldn't you be happy that we caught the bad guy? My job is to catch the bad people, and your friends, your family and Victim Services are there to offer you support. I couldn't believe what I was hearing. The position of Victim Services Liaison wasn't the best match for me.

That old question assailed me. Can police officers perform their duties, see to their own personal safety and also display sensitivity and compassion? I don't know if that's possible, especially with the support and resources that many police agencies currently have or don't have in place. The last thing the public wants is a bunch of emotional police officers on the streets. The public wants and needs police with professional composure. Police officers need to be the calm ones in emergency and life-threatening situations. We are required to be the voice of reason when chaos is breaking out, and the voice of reason does not mix with emotion. We turn our emotions off, but they stay off for so long that we forget how to turn them back on again.

A friend of mine has a young son, six years old, who has hit that stage in his life when he wants to have his friends sleep over. His birthday is coming up, and so my friend agreed to allow him to invite friends from school. There is a boy in his class whose parents are both police officers, and the first thing they said when my friend's son mentioned the sleepover was, "We don't sleep over at other people's houses."

Police officers *know* what goes on at other people's houses. Lots of police officers don't take their children to sit on Santa's knee, because *that ain't Santa and my kid is not sitting on any strange man's knee.* Scouts? Forget it. An RCMP officer who worked on the Child Exploitation Unit had a young daughter. This member started listening through the door when her husband gave their daughter a bath, because her job filled her mind with images and real-life events that made her doubt her own husband's intentions toward their child.

We get so used to living in that state that we don't even consider living any other way. And we don't just maintain that state at work, we bring it home. We don't like anyone and we don't trust anyone. We know it doesn't feel good, but we don't know how to change it, and many come to a point where they give up. Some just check out mentally and emotionally, and others, far too many others, end up taking their own lives. No police officer deserves to feel so overwhelmed with life that suicide seems the only option. No person, especially those who have dedicated their lives to serving others, deserves to live or die feeling that they've been swallowed up by the pain and suffering of the human condition.

So there I was, working with Victim Services. Anne, the coordinator, advised me that the board met once a month and that I really wouldn't have to do much other than attend. As the coordinator of the program, Anne supervised several volunteers called Victim Services Advocates, who attend a scene if required to help a victim's family.

I liked Anne. She understood the police officer's role and her role, and she wasn't trying to mix the two. She was very good at her job and related to victims well, but she was also able to relate to the members. To my great surprise, I gradually became friends with a victim services worker.

The new detachment commander arrived. Despite all the negative talk surrounding her coming, I was optimistic on first impression. Apparently keen on developing positive relationships and a team atmosphere, she purchased a detachment barbecue. We all helped assemble it, then everyone stayed for hamburgers.

A few months later, an incident on duty would change my life.

———

I was working a shift with another member, who picked up a call regarding a motor vehicle accident on a secondary highway. A vehicle had struck a moose. In a departure from the norm, there were no injuries to the occupants of the car. When a vehicle collides with a moose (a bull may weigh up to 1,800 pounds), the result can be fatal for both animal and humans. The vehicle— usually travelling at 80 kilometres an hour or more and often in the dark—strikes the moose in the legs, causing the animal to flip up and either go through the windshield or land on the roof. When I worked as an insurance adjuster in Prince George, I saw the carnage from several moose accidents. The vehicle was often destroyed and the occupants either killed or seriously injured. The only one hurt in this particular accident was the moose.

The moose was lying in the ditch when we arrived on the scene. The poor creature's head was up, but it was obviously unable to walk. This was a tough one for an animal lover like me. The humane thing to do in this circumstance was to dispatch the animal. The other member grabbed the shotgun we brought from the detachment and headed toward it. Before leaving the detachment, my colleague had been unable to find shotgun slugs and instead brought a handful of SSG shots, or buckshot. Buckshot is capable of hitting multiple targets, but with limited power. A slug shot, on the other hand, is one big metal ball that can penetrate hard surfaces—such as a moose's skull.

The moose was large, with a huge rack. The mighty had fallen, and it was sad to behold. Civilians on the scene offered their opinions on the best place to shoot it and put it out of its misery (and me out of mine). I don't care to relive the whole experience; it was terrible. My colleague shot the moose once, then again. We could all see the condensation of its breath filling the air above its nostrils. I couldn't watch anymore. Death by buckshot was like death by stoning; the creature suffered far longer than it should have.

After everyone was certain that the moose was dead, the driver of the vehicle that hit it asked if it would be all right if he slit its throat and bled it out so he could come back later with his truck, take it home and butcher it. I could never be a hunter. There's something about animals and children. I don't know if it's their innocence, but it bothers me so much when they suffer.

I walked back to the police car and sat in the passenger seat. There, I noticed that my ears were ringing. Neither one of us had had any hearing protection from the several shotgun blasts. The only time I had ever discharged a firearm was at the range where hearing protection was available and mandatory—whether you were shooting or just observing. Something felt wrong, but I assumed it was just the whole situation that had me rattled. Eventually, the other member drove us back to the detachment, and I waited for the shift to be over.

Ringing in my ears was not entirely new to me. In Prince George, I had noticed some ringing, faint and intermittent. But the day after the incident with the moose, the ringing was still there and much louder than anything I had ever experienced. I assumed that damage had been done, but I'd been injured before and had always recovered. It would just take a little time. I was having difficulty hearing, but if the ringing would just stop, I told myself, I would be able to hear normally.

Months passed, however, and the ringing persisted. Finally, I saw my family doctor, who referred me to an ear specialist in Edmonton. That doctor examined my ears and then performed an audiogram—a hearing test—that offered immediate results. I was told that I had suffered permanent hearing damage and would not benefit from any treatment—surgery, drugs or hearing aids. Although there was a significant drop in my hearing at the higher frequency levels, the doctor nonetheless believed I could still perform my regular duties.

I remained convinced that if I could rid myself of the ringing, my hearing would return to normal. In my mind, it was the ringing that was keeping me from hearing, not hearing loss.

I decided to advise the RCMP Health Services of my situation. In May 2004, I made an appointment to see one of the Health Services Officers (HSO)—physicians hired by the RCMP to manage and help members with their health issues. I believed Health Services at the RCMP would have access to specialists and that they would spare no expense to "fix me." The HSO has final say, and their decisions about members can override any operational decisions made by detachment commanders or even higher-ranking officers.

During my appointment, I explained to the doctor what had happened and that I had seen a specialist, but he—like the other specialist—offered no solution to my problem. The results of his audiogram were exactly the same as the other one, and the HSO now delivered the devastating news. I was H4. The doctor showed me a copy of the RCMP policy. In RCMP language, an H1, H2 or H3 is considered operational, and an H4 is non-operational or administrative duties only, with H5 the lowest rating possible.

I was stunned. I had possessed better hearing than most of my fellow cadets when I entered training at Depot. Most were H2; I was H1. I asked the doctor what the ramifications would be for my job.

"You wouldn't be able to interview someone who would be potentially violent," he replied.

When I asked why not, he explained that my non-operational status would preclude me from wearing my uniform, and everything that went with it, including, most important, a gun or any protective equipment.

What I suddenly realized was that my career—my life—as a police officer was on the verge of ending. I had left my detachment for the HSO office that day in a police car and wearing the uniform I had worn for eight years. I had no idea it would be the last time I would ever do either of those things. That was my new reality—which didn't seem "real" at all. But one thing was certain. I wouldn't go down without a fight.

My own family doctor's main concern was my long-term hearing. I was thirty-one years old and I now had the hearing of an elderly person. Being a good doctor, she worried that I could further damage my hearing. She wanted me to take the necessary steps to figure out if my hearing loss was steadily decreasing for some unknown reason. I was leaning toward the short term and the immediate effect on my career. What she was advocating made sense: she was thinking long term.

At one point, the audiologist's booth began to feel like a

second home. I worried that the tinnitus—the incessant ringing in my ears—would plague me for the rest of my life. And indeed it has. I still have it today, and the only respite comes when I work with horses or meditate. During those times, the ringing is there but somehow not bothersome.

After one particular round of tests that seemed to indicate a serious decline, I was terrified. What if I was slowly losing my hearing? As I write these words so many years later, the feeling of total devastation I experienced then washes over me again. My genuine surprise at the results of those tests left me unable to disguise my overwhelming disappointment from anger, and so the tears flowed. I left the office and walked across the parking lot to my car. I sat there for a long time feeling very lost . . . and tired.

After that particular appointment, I was supposed to drive back to Redwater for the remainder of my shift. When I came to the turnoff, I elected instead to pull over to the side of the road. I didn't want to go to the office. I knew that my detachment commander would be on me as soon as I walked through the door. She hadn't said anything to me, but other members at the detachment had told me she believed I was faking it. I was reminded on a regular basis that my being off the shift rotation forced other members to carry my weight. I decided to call her and tell her that I needed to go home. I had a significant amount of vacation time saved up, and I just needed some time to regroup.

I remember hearing her voice on the phone and closing my eyes. I thought, Just get through it. She asked straight out what the results of the test were, and I reluctantly told her that it appeared I was slowly losing my hearing and that I was having some anxiety about gradually going deaf. I explained that I would like the rest of the week off to figure out what the hell I was going to do. She denied my request. She told me I needed to go to work, and she had things for me to do. We argued briefly, and finally, she told me to go home for the rest of the day, but added that she expected me back in the office the next morning.

I ended the call and sat there in my car, knowing that I was about to embark on the fight of my life. I would be fighting for my hearing and to keep my identity as a police officer—a Mountie. Help was not coming. I was on my own. I needed to stop being sad and start getting mad, because it was the only way I would be able to make it through.

I started a process of documentation. I had a bad feeling about what was transpiring, and I knew that documentation would be the only way to preserve what was happening. In part, I was processing what was happening. The grievance I had lodged over the staffing issue was a twisted path, and so was the struggle to resolve my hearing issue. As I was a trained RCMP investigator, the habit of writing up a case was deeply engrained. Investigation was all about documenting. Sometimes I would be somewhere and have time to write something down on a piece of paper, which I would then toss into the book.

In addition to noting dates and times, I was writing what turned into more of a journal. I had kept one in my youth, and I had done so at Depot, but my workload as an RCMP officer had been more demanding. There had been no time in recent years. Now I went back to the practice. Initially I had a running log on my computer at work. Then at home, I started a more personal and intimate journal that contained more than just the facts. The diaries would turn out to be useful as I wrote this book (though I have to say that rereading those pages was painful). And at the time, the journals served another purpose: they allowed me to vent and to clear my head of some of the garbage that was gathering there. I look back at those diaries now and see how angry I was. The language is searing and raw.

In my heart of hearts, I knew that both the grievance and the hearing issue were going to go badly. I felt my detachment commander's behaviour toward me change. She went from calling me into her office to say she wanted to further my career to not allowing me to have coffee with my colleagues. They were operational, she declared, and I was not.

Over the next few months, my hearing appeared to be deteriorating at a disturbing and unexplainable rate. The doctor was unable to offer any theories, solutions or advice. I had so many questions, and nobody seemed to have any answers. A series of audiograms consistently revealed that I had some minor damage to the lower frequencies, but several higher frequencies had plummeted. The graph looked like a steep drop down a mountainside and seemed to offer clear evidence that one event—the shotgun blast—was to blame.

As far as Health Services was concerned, it was pretty cut and dried. My operational career was over. But I wasn't ready to give up. I was working hard to find something that would help, but when he told me my operational status would remain unchanged, it just hit me all over again.

I was attached to my identity as a police officer. Although I didn't always agree with the way the RCMP handled things, I honestly couldn't imagine myself doing anything else. When I looked at myself in the mirror, I saw a police officer.

Much later, I came across the work of Amy Cuddy, an American social psychologist at Harvard University who has written extensively about body language and power, among other things. When she was an undergrad, Cuddy was in a terrible car accident and suffered a serious head injury. Before the injury, she had been labelled gifted, but after the accident, doctors told her that her IQ had dropped by two standard deviations, that this loss was likely permanent and that she would face major challenges in completing her undergraduate degree. It was suggested that maybe university wasn't the best route for her anymore. Cuddy eventually did recover (and complete both an MA and a PhD at Princeton). She mentioned during her TED Talks presentation that she had "identified" with being smart. And when her core identity was taken away, "nothing makes you feel more powerless." As much as I was interested in her research about body language, it was her comment about feeling powerless as a result of losing her identity that really caught my attention.

Cuddy and her colleagues have done research to show that by simply adopting power poses (even for as little as two minutes), both men and women can increase the levels of testosterone in their bodies and decrease the level of cortisol—a stress hormone. Change the body, change the mind.

Even in horses, frame of body equals frame of mind. Change a horse's body by massaging its head down or by bending the body from side to side to release stiffness and tension; the horse's mind will soon follow. It's not a permanent solution to what are normally complex issues, but it can put a horse in a place where he doesn't feel so stressed and unsure.

It also works in the reverse—frame of mind equals frame of body. When one's mind becomes accustomed to believing it's constantly under threat, it sends the signals in the body to stay alert. It becomes a cycle that is difficult to break. The more your body's stress system is activated, the harder it is to turn it off. Self-awareness, mindfulness, diet and exercise are proven ways to effectively manage stress. Change the body or change the mind, and the rest will follow.

———

I won't go into all the details, but suffice to say I saw little compassion or understanding coming from the RCMP during this difficult time. The audiologist had documented that stress and fatigue would worsen the ringing. I was hardly sleeping by then. I'm a quiet person and I like my quiet time. The only problem was that I could never have quiet time again, because the ringing was all day, every day.

I was struggling, trying to find a way to cope. I was a mess physically, emotionally and mentally. My family doctor put me on medical leave for two months, starting in June 2004, to allow me to find the medical answers I was seeking and also to provide some relief from the pressures coming from all sides at work. The RCMP's staff relations rep, for example, called me and told me it would be in my best interests to go back to work before being ordered back to work. To do otherwise, he said, would look bad on my record.

My commanding officer, meanwhile, ordered me to go back to the Health Services Officer. She was convinced I should not be on medical leave for the hearing injury and the linked depression that I was suffering. The biggest battle of all was with her. One minute she seemed to understand the severity of the effects of my injury; the next minute she was threatening me with a Code of Conduct investigation for disobeying her orders to revisit the HSO. That truly shocked and dismayed me. Again, I felt betrayed.

I did meet with the HSO, and I felt I had to return to work or would have been ordered to. So I did, in July 2004, much to my family's dismay. I was referred by the Return to Work Coordinator to the Member/Employee Assistance Program (MEAP), which could connect me to outside medical assistance. (MEAP has recently been replaced with a 1-800-number referral program.) However, I chose not to use MEAP as I was already accessing medical care through my own personal doctor but, more importantly I was concerned about confidentiality given that MEAP was staffed by other members.

Back at work, I was crumbling, and my family doctor was advising me to seek proper treatment to make sure I didn't come crashing down.

I became the focus of a family intervention. My husband and other family members were adamant that I must follow my doctor's instructions and take the full medical leave for my depression. They knew better than to tell me the blunt truth: I was falling apart and needed help. They were convinced that I would either react with anger or simply move deeper into myself to prove that nothing was wrong. Their tactic was to tell me that if I went against my own doctor, she would probably choose to not support me for the remainder of this process. I would end up alienating a medical professional who had a true and vested interest in my health. We also talked about how this was all affecting me—my sleep and my memory—and the fact that I was self-medicating by using alcohol to calm myself and help me fall asleep. I knew they were right.

I see photographs now of my daughter at that time, and I can't remember those moments. It's like I wasn't even there, and really, I wasn't. I may have been there in body, but my mind was far too busy. This period of my life was filled with fight after fight—fighting to return to operational duty, fighting endlessly with my supervisor, fighting to get hearing aids, fighting about who would pay for them. It seemed the fighting would never stop.

———

Things at the detachment continued to get worse. I had decided that I would give my firearm, firearm magazines, pepper spray and expandable baton to the corporal at Redwater Detachment for what I trusted would be safekeeping, to avoid having to surrender them on demand to my detachment commander.

One day, I went into the change room and retrieved from my locker the black gun case that I had been issued at Depot. My gun belt was hanging from the hook inside. I laid it all out on the bench. First, I pulled out the expandable baton and set it on the bench. Next, I unsnapped the flap that held my pepper spray in place. I pulled the canister out, shook it to see how much was left and placed it next to my baton. Next, I unsnapped the buttons and released my two extra ammunition magazines.

Feeling their weight in my hands made me think about Depot. My hands are so small that I was trained on the small version of the 9mm Smith & Wesson. Its magazine was considerably smaller than the regular-sized one. When I qualified on the range to return to work in Prince George, the instructor insisted I try the larger 9mm. It was bigger and held several more rounds, which might just come in handy one day. From that day on, I carried that model on my belt.

And last, I unfastened the snaps to my firearm. I pulled it out and, with my right thumb, pushed the magazine release button like I'd done a hundred times before. I grabbed the magazine with my left hand and placed it on the bench. My gun was always loaded, which meant there was still one bullet in the chamber. I racked the slide and heard that metal-on-metal sound that I can hear clearly even now. The bullet was ejected, and I picked it up and placed it on the grey foam that lined the inside of my gun case. I gave a small smile as I looked at the engraved horse and Mountie on the side of the barrel. The empty gun was considerably lighter in my hands, which were now shaking.

I quickly placed everything neatly in the case, determined to stay focused. One last look and I closed the case and locked it. I walked into the office of my corporal, who was surprised when I presented the case and its contents. I explained that I would rather do this on my terms and that I would be back for them at some point. But more than just equipment was left in that office in that case that day.

I was grateful to have the support of the other frontline members at the detachment; however, management was a completely different story. I still have in my possession pages and pages of daily incidents that I perceived to be harassing in nature, not only related to my hearing loss. Seemingly arbitrary rules were made that applied only to me. I was methodically isolated from the other members at the detachment. It got to a point where it was announced during a detachment meeting that if I didn't return to operational duty, it would be my fault that some members would not be granted leave at Christmas and New Year's. Instead of jumping on board to make my life even more difficult, the members were a source of support and motivation. They took offence at the way I was being treated. Unfortunately, this all made for a tense and often hostile environment. They paid a price, but never waned in their sense of morality and justice. And for that I will be forever grateful.

In another effort to right all the wrongs I felt were being done to me, I filed a harassment complaint against my detachment commander. My initial complaint listed numerous incidents that I perceived as harassment.

———

There came a point when I stopped doing all the things that gave me pleasure, because I just didn't have the energy. I started to go deeper and deeper into myself. Any sort of effort to communicate with anyone else, including my family, was more than I could handle. I could only manage the basics, such as putting one foot in front of the other.

About a year later, I had an appointment with my family doctor. These appointments were a treasured time. Waiting for my doctor in the examination rooms, I would sit in the chair at the far end, facing the door. I would lean my head back onto the wall and close my eyes. For me, the examination room was a resting

place, quiet (as quiet as it would ever be again) and safe. My doctor would knock on the door, which signalled me to open my
eyes, and she would come in.

On this visit, her first comment was how terrible I looked.
I told her everything that had happened since my last appointment. She asked me a question that I wasn't expecting. She asked
if I was having suicidal thoughts. No, I said. But I added that
I wasn't entirely convinced I was above hurting someone else,
especially someone who was making my life and others' lives difficult. I was also having very violent dreams.

She asked me if I was depressed. I didn't like the "D" word and
didn't want to have any part of it. *Depressed* would mean weak,
and I wasn't weak. She told me that my opinion was typical of
most professional people, and she suggested I do some research
and educate myself on the topic. Depression, she explained, is a
chemical imbalance in the brain and a condition I had absolutely
no control over. Great. Another thing in my life I had no control
over. She wanted to prescribe me antidepressants, but I declined.
I was determined to will my way out of it.

She advised me that she was obligated to put me on medical
leave, the third one in two years. The first, in June, had lasted a
few weeks; this one would last about three months. My doctor
said she couldn't return me to work—a place where things could
escalate to a point where someone might be harmed. She handed
me the name of a psychologist. Then she handed me the paperwork I would have to give to my detachment commander. My
doctor wrote on it that she was booking me off for an indeter-
minate amount of time for the purpose of pursuing therapy
related to my tinnitus and for "treatment of depression."

I took the paperwork and left her office. I should have felt a tremendous relief, but I didn't. The walk to my car felt like the walk of shame. I knew I probably needed to talk to someone, but with the "D" word out there for everyone to see, and with me starting to see a psychologist, my career would be over for sure.

Over the next few weeks, I found myself admitting to having intensely violent dreams, and I told my psychologist about some incidents from my policing past that were becoming increasingly bothersome. Memories from my first posting, in particular, seemed to be stuck in my brain. I had noticed them before, but there was always something else to preoccupy me: another call or an effort to salvage my career. Both had kept me from dwelling on these moments.

Now that there was no other call, now that I was removed from having to deal with my detachment commander, these memories and images made their way to the surface and would not be denied their moments at centre stage. I felt too tired. I didn't have the energy to shove them back down anymore. They were the images I went to sleep with, they were there when I slept at night, and they were there when I woke up. This, my second medical leave, went on for approximately three months before I returned back to work against the recommendations of my doctor. In addition to the pressure I felt from the organization, my own shame and fear were getting the best of me. As stressful as it was to be at work, my self-imposed embarrassment and fear of dealing with my depression was overwhelming in comparison. In total, I took four paid medical leaves from the RCMP between 2004 and 2009, trying to come to terms with my issues.

My battles with the RCMP over the grievance and how I was treated in the wake of the hearing injury would last several years. The staffing grievance was dismissed as I was said to be suitably posted to meet the needs of the Redwater Detachment. The harassment complaint was ultimately dismissed. It was ruled as simply a "workplace conflict." My next step was to go to the Canadian Human Rights Commission.

I could no longer hear sounds in the higher frequencies, but there was one thing I would eventually come to hear perfectly well: a whisper that said, *You're good at police work, but is it good for you?* It was as if a higher power were taking away my hearing in order to get me to listen.

CHAPTER SEVEN

A Lesson in Self-Awareness

A s the impact of my work grew, and my body and spirit began to wear down, I expected some compassion from the RCMP for what I was going through. As far as I was concerned, I got none.

The Alberta Union of Provincial Employees (AUPE) recently initiated research—independently carried out through the University of Calgary—into the high turnover rate of social workers in the province. AUPE anticipated that the results would show that social workers are exposed to so much trauma and so many difficult situations that involve children that it all just becomes too much. The preliminary results showed something contrary to what was expected. It wasn't traumatic events that caused the most psychological and emotional damage, but a negative workplace environment.

Most of the time, I could handle what I saw and experienced as a police officer. It was the feeling of being betrayed by the RCMP that caused the most hurt. I had bought into the notion that the force was family, and while I didn't always like the family, I did think they would take care of me if need be. You are broken down in training and made to believe in the camaraderie, but no one tells you that it's conditional. And when that breach of trust and that abandonment hit you, it's hard to find your way through.

By 2009, I was a thirteen-year veteran of the force, and I had been battling the RCMP on several fronts and losing most of the time. I had launched a complaint against a detachment commander for what I viewed as harassment, which was dismissed. I had launched a complaint with the Canadian Human Rights Commission over the way an injury I'd suffered on the job—loss of hearing—had been handled, which was settled. Time after time, I had asked for help from the RCMP, and each time I was denied. Finally, I came to grasp a hard truth: I was on my own.

If I had died on that bridge in Prince George, I would have been honoured in a way that few people are. Had I been killed in the line of duty, my funeral and the ceremonies that followed would have been those of a hero. But I survived that day and many others, so why wasn't I being honoured by my organization in life as I would have been in death?

As I see it, this is the heart of the dysfunction in the RCMP. Many leaders in the organization no longer seem to have compassion for the rank and file or for the public. RCMP managers are well versed in the appropriate things to say, but few act on those words. They ask us to perform our duties with an integrity, honesty, professionalism, compassion, respect and accountability (all core values listed on the RCMP website) that they seem incapable of themselves. Their words say one thing, their actions another—leading to confusion, frustration and anger among members. The hardest part is that most individuals in the RCMP aren't even aware of the inconsistency.

———

As police officers, we are conscious of other people's body language, scanning for signs of innocence or guilt. But are we as officers aware of our own body language? I know I often wasn't. Once you become aware of yourself and what you are projecting, you begin to understand the direct effect you have on those around you.

Working with horses would offer me a critical lesson in awareness—paying attention and recognizing the different body language that horses "speak" but that humans don't understand. Horses do not hide how they feel about you and what you are doing in their presence. Tail swishing, ears pinned back, head high or low—all these mean something specific.

And there was a bigger lesson. I was to become aware of what *I* was doing with *my* body language. I was responsible for the energy that I was bringing with me to the horse and for the reactions I was eliciting. What a relief, for a change, to have instant, honest and genuine feedback.

Up to that point, I had spent much time and precious energy trying to remain one step ahead of those I was dealing with in the RCMP. I was constantly reading between the lines of every email and every conversation I had with anyone from the RCMP. I spent my days and nights calculating and manoeuvring—convincing myself that I had some control over my outcome. If I just played my cards right and continued to do the right thing, I told myself, everything would work out.

I found the horses, on the other hand, so incredibly refreshing—and easy—to be around. And each horse was different, so I
had to pay attention and be in the moment, constantly evaluat-
ing and changing what I was doing in order to produce the best
result. It all made perfect sense.

———

I had gone to Riversong Ranch in 2009 for two reasons. I needed
help developing a relationship with Maggie, and I also had
thoughts about implementing some sort of a program involving horses and aimed at members suffering from post-traumatic stress disorder and other job-induced trauma. Riversong
is owned and operated by two gifted and knowledgeable horse
trainers, Chris Irwin and Kathryn Kincannon. What I learned
from the two of them is how to play horse games by horse rules.
Having a background in observing body language in people, I
found the concept of horse body language intriguing.

At this point in my policing career, I was working in the
RCMP's commercial crime unit in Edmonton. I held the mistaken view that I was in good shape. My hearing loss and tinnitus
still plagued me, but mentally and emotionally, I thought I was
on an even keel.

Trauma, I would come to understand, lives in both the brain
and the body. Finding a way to connect with the horses opened
up a path to coping with my own psychological damage. And
working with my own horse, Maggie, would teach me so many
lessons, the biggest one being the true meaning of forgiveness.

———

Most horse farms have at least one round pen—a 15-metre-wide enclosure where trainers typically do ground work. That is, they work with the horse not from the saddle but from the ground. The round pen could also be called the communication zone. It's a place where communication is constant between horse and human. The ideal situation is for one person to be in the middle, while a calm and content thousand-pound animal walks or trots clockwise or counter-clockwise around the perimeter. Round pens vary in size: they are always small enough that interaction is inevitable but large enough for things to get completely out of control due to inadvertent miscommunications between person and horse.

I remember stepping into the round pen the first time with Maggie. My friend Shelley had entered with her first to provide me with a little demonstration. With a whip in her hand, she took her spot in the middle of the pen and used her body and the motion of the whip to send Maggie off in the direction she was already facing. Shelley explained what she was doing as my mare trotted in circles around her. She was keeping her core or belly aimed at Maggie's hip and using the whip (without making contact) to keep Maggie in motion. She said it was important to watch the horse's tail and ears, which signal her mood and intention. It would be a bad thing if the horse turned her hind end in, comparable to giving someone the middle finger.

I wasn't entirely sure I wanted to try it out myself, but it looked easy enough. All I had to do was stand in the middle of the pen and follow her around with my belly pointed to her hip. The physical aspect of it wasn't the issue. The issue was putting myself into a confined space with an animal I didn't trust. I found horses to be unpredictable and, to be honest, a little crazy. They lose their minds when they get scared or spooked. It becomes fight or flight as they abandon all sense; they will run through a barbwire fence if something as small as a falling leaf happens to startle them. The whole concept of being in a small ring with such a flighty creature ran counter to everything I had been living and breathing—small spaces and crazy bad guys, I well knew, were incompatible.

I watched from outside the pen, and I was impressed as Shelley brought Maggie to a halt simply by taking a few steps backwards. Maggie stopped trotting, turned her head and brought her body in toward Shelley. Okay, I thought, that was pretty cool. Shelley asked if I wanted to try. She offered to stay in the pen with me and help me with my positioning and the motion of the whip. It was a good opportunity to learn, and Maggie and I desperately needed a bonding experience. I had only had her for about a month or so, and our "relationship" was already strained. She was not the easygoing, get-up-and-ride-her-into-the-sunset kind of horse that I had envisioned. We needed to have a positive experience in order for both of us to become motivated to improve our relationship.

I opened the gate of the pen and walked into the centre, where Shelley was standing. When I looked at Maggie, she turned her head away, licked her lips and then turned her head back to stare straight at me.

My eyes flashed Maggie a warning: *don't you dare turn your ass in toward me, because I know what it means.* Shelley passed me the whip and gave me some instructions. When ready, I was to put up my left hand to block Maggie from coming in and, with the whip in my right hand, send her from me and around the pen. I took a deep breath and successfully put Maggie into motion.

There seemed to be so much to think about. I had to remember to block with my left hand while keeping the whip moving in my right hand and taking small steps to follow Maggie around the pen. I had to make sure my belly was aimed toward her hip, all the while watching her tail and ears. After a few minutes, Shelley said to stop her, and we took a couple of steps backwards, bringing Maggie's head and body toward the centre of the pen. Shelley then stepped outside the pen and took a spectator spot, viewing Maggie and me through the spaces in the wooden planks.

Another deep breath and I sent Maggie into motion once more. I could hear the pounding of her hooves on the dirt and the slap of tiny rocks on the tops of those hooves as she went around and around. The sounds she made—blowing air out of her nose and mouth, and her hooves hitting the dirt—were all I heard. I knew we were in a pen, but I didn't see the boards, only this beautiful golden mare. After a few minutes, I stopped Maggie by stepping backwards. She took it easy on me and turned in headfirst, whereupon we stared at each other for a moment. I walked over to the gate, exited the pen and said to Shelley, "That was awesome!"

It's possible I was reacting to the fact that I'd decided to step into a situation I wasn't comfortable with and had come out unscathed. Or maybe it was just that I had tried something new. Part of the wonder of the experience was having this powerful animal running around me "free"—but there was something else. I knew that Maggie and I hadn't necessarily had *our* moment, but I had had a moment of my own. I had found the session absolutely

exhilarating. Round penning had been empowering for more reasons than one. I knew I had to learn more.

————

The next time I was in a round pen was at Riversong Ranch in
2010. My first day at this second clinic, I volunteered to go into the
pen with a horse named Razzy. I asked what I was expected to do
with this beautiful black Thoroughbred, and Chris and Kathryn,
coaching from a spot nearby, said, "Do whatever comes naturally."

It's hard to resist petting a horse. I went to his shoulder,
which is what I had learned through some videos I had seen.
Most people's first instinct is to go to the head of a horse, but in
reality the face is the *last* place the horse wants you to touch. I
approached Razzy's shoulder, his head facing off to my left and
his rear to my right. I was asked to stroke Razzy again and to
notice anything in his body language. I touched him with my left
hand again, and immediately there was a swish of his tail. Just
one single swish, perceptible to everyone watching. Translation:
*I don't find you completely offensive, but what you're doing annoys
me just a bit.*

I was asked to stroke Razzy once more, and sure enough,
another swish. Chris suggested another try, this time changing
the hand I used. I turned slightly and reached out to pet him, this
time with my right hand. No swish. It was my first real lesson in
body language. Not just the body language of the horse, but how
I was responsible for my own. Why would switching from left to
right make such a difference to that horse? It had to do with my
left hand entering the space closest to the horse's head. To pet
him with my left hand, I had to either reach across my body or

turn my body in to the horse. Not so with the right hand. In that moment, now armed with that small insight into body language, my issues with Maggie became clear. She was reacting to me, and I, in turn, was reacting to her reaction, and it was escalating to the point of frustration for both of us. It was so simple and yet so complicated.

I was immediately drawn to Razzy. And once I learned more about him, I understood why. He is an ex-racehorse from a track in Kentucky. If you believe, as I do, that horses can be traumatized, then he, too, was coping with post-traumatic stress disorder. He had been raised and trained to perform a certain function, and he would do his job as required or he would suffer the consequences. And if, for some reason, he could no longer do his job, he would be tossed aside like garbage and another just like him would take his place.

The next day at the clinic, we learned how to lunge a horse. The lunging exercise is similar to the round pen exercise, except the horse wears a halter and is connected to his handler by a twenty-foot-long rope called a lunge line. This almost always takes place in the ample confines of a riding arena or a paddock. In lunging, as in the round pen exercise, the horse walks, trots or canters in a circle around you as you hold the line in one hand and a whip in the other. Again, the whip is not used for contact, but motioned across the horse's body from back to front, to keep him moving forward. A calm, level whip encourages forward momentum, while high or erratic use of the whip is seen by the horse as aggressive and confusing.

In the horse's eyes, the whip is an extension of my arm and mimics the body of another horse, allowing me to communicate with the horse in his own language. The core of my body is also a source of communication, and it can often conflict with what my mind and the rest of my body are trying to say. Again, it felt like there was so much to think about—I was to keep my shoulder out of the path of the horse's head, lead with my outside foot, open my hip, maintain my core fixed on the horse's shoulder (as opposed to his hip), and keep the whip level with a back to front motion.

Every part of my body had its own job to do, including watching what the horse was doing. I had to monitor and assess his tail, ears, barrel and the level of his head (high, low, in between). If anything in the horse's body showed signs of stress, irritation or non-compliance, I needed to reassess my own body and make any necessary adjustments. It was complicated, but I felt up to the challenge.

I was partnered up that day with a small black Mustang named Peek-a-Boo, rather than Razzy. Everyone in the arena started off working with his or her respective horse in hand. Despite the fact that I hadn't worked with Peek-a-Boo before, it didn't take long for us to become comfortable with each other. Chris saw our progress and suggested we go ahead and start the lunging exercise.

Although I had spent some time in the round pen, I had never lunged a horse before, and I felt a degree of apprehension. With the rope in my left hand and the whip in my right hand, I did my best to send Peek off in a counter-clockwise circle. He looked like he would set off without a hitch, only to stop after a couple of steps.

After a few more unsuccessful attempts to get Peek moving, Chris came over and suggested we start off facing each other. A push to Peek's shoulder and a step forward, and away he went. I ran through my mental checklist, starting with my feet and moving up to my shoulders, but before I could finish, Peek came to an unexpected halt. I managed to send him off again in the same direction. I heard a voice from behind me, telling me to watch my core and that I was getting ahead of him. I looked down and confirmed that my core (my belly button) was no longer pointed at Peek's shoulder, but at his head.

I adjusted, and we continued to go around and around. Peek-a-Boo and I now found our rhythm. Actually more than just rhythm: we were in perfect alignment. And for whatever reason, I allowed myself to surrender to the moment. When I use the term *surrender*, I do not do so lightly. *Surrender* is not a normal word in my vocabulary. I hate losing, and as a police officer the word *surrender* had come to mean more than just losing.

I wondered for a long time whether I had surrendered on that bridge in Prince George. Was the inability to move and react a sign of giving up? It wasn't until I heard Dr. Jacqui Linder speak that I understood what had happened. Dr. Linder is an Edmonton psychologist whose PhD dissertation was on soul loss in survivors of childhood sexual abuse. She has spoken widely at police colleges and to gatherings of first responders on the neurobiology of PTSD, stress and burnout, and she attended the War Horse Symposium in 2011 as a guest.

Most people believe that a threat engages a fight-or-flight response in a person; in fact, there are three possible responses—fight, flight or *freeze*. While I was on the bridge, my brain involuntarily jumped into this primitive mode of survival, and instead of responding with fight or even flight, it locked into freeze. I have no doubt that once one of those men had put his hands on me, the fight would have been on. Unfortunately, if I'm realistic about my situation, my size and strength put me at a distinct disadvantage. As the threat closed the space between us, my chances of survival quickly faded.

I had tools on my belt that are effective—at a distance. I'm quick and I'm accurate, but neither is helpful when two people are right on top of me. At that point, the tools designed to save my life—my pepper spray, my expandable baton and my gun—became weapons that others could use to end it.

Hearing this information from Dr. Linder and comprehending that I had no control over my response allowed me to forgive myself. I did not *choose* to do nothing. I am not a coward, or useless. If anything, I was caught being complacent. All police officers know that complacency is what can get you hurt—which is why we opt for hypervigilance. Our options are to run the risk of being hurt or killed, or be on guard every day, all day.

But what is the difference between what we call "being alert" and living in a constant state of fear? It's exactly the same for the horses. They live in a constant state of fear that some predator is going to jump out from the bushes and attack them. Whether that threat is real or perceived, it's what occupies their minds. And when I began to fathom what it means to a horse to be spared that fear and vulnerability (at least for the time I am with him), I couldn't help but wonder how I could do that for myself. And what it would mean to share that insight with others.

As Peek-a-Boo and I went around and around in circles, I sensed in one magical moment his sudden relaxation and loss of fear. I could feel the transfer of energy between the two of us and felt the wave as it rippled through his body. When it was over, I couldn't wait to do it again. My mind tried to refute what had just happened, but I could not ignore the feeling. That's what working with horses does: the experience provokes not only thoughts but feelings.

I cannot and will not deny what I saw and felt that day. For a long time, I was convinced that it would serve no purpose to share my experience of that moment. People, I believed, need to have their own experiences in order to understand and relate.

The next day I chose to work with Razzy. If any horse could go there with me to that place I had been with Peek-a-Boo, I thought it would be Razzy. I began lunging him at the far end of the arena. After we lined up face to face, I took a step forward and to the right, and with a level whip in my right hand, I sent Razzy off in a counter-clockwise direction. In that moment with Peek-a-Boo, I felt calm and quiet. I still had problems with my hearing from the on-the-job injury that had left me with constant high-pitched ringing in my ears, but in that moment all was silent. I had found my moment of peace—and my quiet—and I wanted to go back there as soon as possible.

But then Razzy began to stop at the same spot in the circle, over and over. I asked one of the other participants if he could watch for a minute and help me figure out what was causing the horse to react in that way. I had already done my mental checklist, and it seemed as though my body was saying all the right things.

Once more I sent Razzy off, and he continued to stop each time he did the circle, growing increasingly agitated. The person watching couldn't see any miscommunication on my part and could not offer any sort of explanation or assistance. I had been so ready to repeat the magical experience I'd had with Peek, but Razzy and I could not have been less in sync.

Yet I sent him off again, convinced for some reason that this time would be different from the last six or seven times. Same result. But this time when Razzy reached that spot in the circle, he reared and then bolted. My natural reaction, of course, was to hang on to the rope, believing that my strength would be enough to regain control. As you can imagine, I was no match for Razzy.

I wasn't wearing gloves and the lunge line ripped through my hands, leaving me with patches of open skin. The sting in my hands was nothing compared to the sting I felt to my pride. I clearly remember Chris's words: "You didn't do anything to cause that to happen, but you didn't do anything to prevent it from happening either."

So desperate was I to have that feeling again, so fixed on the past and so expectant of the future, that I had stopped paying attention. Consumed with what I needed from Razzy, I wasn't paying attention to what Razzy needed from me. I understand now that that connection can only happen when the needs of both, whether people or animals, are being met.

Looking back, I really don't know what was setting Razzy off. Maybe he didn't want to cross another horse's lines (other horses were being worked nearby), or maybe the next person down was working with a mare whom Razzy liked—or disliked. In any case, he needed something from me at the time that I wasn't giving him. I wasn't there in the moment with him. I didn't antici-pate his stopping, and I just let it happen over and over again. My answer to the problem was to "make" him do it. I had become frustrated and angry, so I'm sure the energy I was throwing at him was intense. And in the end, he said *No.*

Still, Razzy remains one of my favourites. Whenever I work with him, he has no problem telling me exactly where I am. If I come into his space with intense energy and an agenda, he wants no part of it. He had years of people coming into his space at the racetrack and pushing their wants and needs upon him, and it stressed him out to the point where he could not be ridden. He reached his limit, and he didn't want to go back to that state—and who could blame him?

I don't want to go back either.

In October of 2009, I was having some major second thoughts about signing up for Kathryn's Equiana workshop, my first at the ranch. Three days with a bunch of women—what was I thinking? One irritating woman could easily make three days seems like three months. My saving grace was that my newly purchased horse, Maggie, was going to make the trip this time. This would be a perfect opportunity to build a solid foundation between us. I was looking forward to feeding her first thing in the morning and having plenty of uninterrupted time to create a bond.

After all the women in the workshop had introduced themselves, Kathryn led us into the arena. Given the nature of this particular workshop (women only), she had decided to include the mares at Riversong. Some of the mares on the property were already together in their paddocks, and others had not been around one another for a while. One mare, Katja, had always been the alpha mare—no matter what other horses were with her. We all grabbed halters and set out to catch five mares from different paddocks on the property.

There were three horses in Katja's paddock. The mare met us at the gate, but the other two horses skedaddled up the hill and into the trees. I offered to stay with Katja at the bottom and wait for the other two horses to be caught. I had never worked with her before, although I had seen some of the more experienced participants in other clinics do so. She takes her job as alpha mare very seriously and does not easily give over that control. I have to say that I was a bit intimated by her, and it didn't take long for her to show me why I felt uneasy.

After her fellow mares ran up the hill, they were no longer in sight, and she didn't like that one bit. She began calling to them, and when I tried to calm her, she put her head down and brought it up suddenly into my abdomen, lifting me off my feet and throwing me backwards. I managed to keep my balance, but she had definitely made her point.

Thankfully, the other women soon caught the other mares, and we made our way into the arena. In the arena already were the younger mares. One was Katja's daughter, Avalon, and another was Ekwa, offspring of Chris's mare, Tsunami. Avalon had inherited her dam's willingness to lead. She was young, but determined to climb the leadership ladder. I found myself still reluctantly hanging onto Katja's lead rope as we entered the arena.

When Katja caught wind of the two youngsters at the other end, she was eager to show them who was boss. And it wasn't me. My instinct was to let this horse go, and get out of the arena myself before all hell broke loose. I reached up and unbuckled her halter, and once she was free, she took off down to the other end of the arena. I quickly made my way to the gate, eager to be on the other side of a high wall.

The horses already in Katja's herd had no interest in challenging her bid to be top mare. They quickly bowed to her and wanted little to do with the two youngsters. It became obvious that her main objective was to get the two juveniles in line, but Avalon and Ekwa were in a rebellious mood. Exchanges between Katja and the young rebels left me holding my breath as Katja attempted to corner the two, spinning and doing her best to line them up to deliver a powerful kick that would surely leave a mark. The youngsters, though, were too quick, and she never made contact.

Amazingly, Katja was not high-headed and out of control, running around, kicking and biting and demanding submission. On the contrary, she was calm—but assertive. At the slightest hint of disrespect from Avalon or Ekwa, she would slowly stalk them with a level head until she was close enough to express her displeasure.

Avalon was the first to reconsider her desire to be the alpha mare. She eventually bowed to Katja and went for a roll in the dirt. Ekwa was now on her own and still believed that she had what it took to be the leader in the group. There followed more physical exchanges, with Katja trying to kick Ekwa into submission and the latter running away, high-headed and determined not to conform.

And then something unexpected and fascinating occurred. Katja approached Ekwa and, instead of using physical force, positioned herself in a different way. Katja stood off to Ekwa's side and wrapped her head underneath and around Ekwa's neck and began to nibble gently at Ekwa's withers. This is what mares do to soothe a foal who has become agitated, so both horses would have been familiar with the gesture. But it was the sudden change in tactics that astonished those of us watching. Katja did this for a while, and we all watched in amazement as Ekwa's head slowly came down, and she relaxed. Katja stopped and straightened herself. The competition was over. Katja had given us all a lesson in true leadership, and we sat there in awe of her.

It made me think about the man in the field outside Brooks, Alberta—the man who wanted me to kill him. During our confrontation, I started off by matching his language and aggression with my own, telling him I would shoot him if need be, but then realizing that this approach was getting me nowhere. Then I relied on instinct and switched tactics. Changing to a somewhat softer approach, I diffused the situation long enough to give me the opportunity to handcuff him and end our standoff.

This was the only time I could think of during my career that I had shown this leadership quality. "My way or the highway" had been my guiding philosophy. I can justify this by saying that I, and police officers in general, need to be in control of every situation. Our lives and others' lives depend on it. Yet I can't help but question that leadership model. Over time, I had become the same type of leader that I had rebelled against and promised myself I would never be.

At the end of that day, we were all asked which horse in that scenario we identified with. Woman after woman identified with Katja. Her strength, power and leadership resonated with more than half the group. They saw themselves as being the same calm and confident leader, with the ability to adjust to the individual needs of another.

The question in my mind was this: Were those the qualities they possessed right then or the ones they *wished* they had? It takes a tremendous amount of effort and energy to be able to assess each person we meet as an individual, but it's what we as individuals all want. We want to be valued and treated as individuals, with specific needs and wants. Which is why I identified with that young but defiant mare, Ekwa.

It was in part her attitude of "don't come in here and tell me what to do and threaten to kick my ass if I don't conform" (sounds familiar). *That might be good enough for those other horses, but that's not good enough for me. If you want me to follow, I need more. In fact, I demand more.* As a result, the standoff and disrespect continue until either the physically stronger prevails or the true leader emerges. The rightful alpha mare had stepped up, and it was an effective reminder of what it takes to be a strong and respected leader. And if given the opportunity again, it was the type of leader I would choose to be.

———

Enter Maggie. As much as I may have been known to push other people's buttons, Maggie was a master at pushing mine. In fact, she didn't just push my buttons, she jumped up and down on them . . . repeatedly. But I was ready, willing and eager to turn a new page. I'd been inspired by Katja and I was up for the challenge to become the leader Maggie needed me to be.

That afternoon, we were to begin by walking in a counter-clockwise direction in the arena with our respective horses, an in-hand exercise. I was at Maggie's left shoulder with my right hand in contact with the lead rope to her halter. If she looked or bent to her right, I would touch her barrel to straighten her out. If she bent to her left, into my space, I would block her with my hand at the corner of her mouth. All the horses test to see if you're paying attention and if you see what they are doing. After you make the appropriate corrections to keep horses straight, they usually relax and put their heads down. I'd done this several times before—piece of cake.

I smiled as we walked around the arena. Then Maggie bent into me, and I responded with the appropriate reaction of a light touch to her barrel to straighten her out. I anticipated her next move as she bent the other way and brought her head into my space: I threw up my block. Then she dropped her shoulder into my hip, pushing me over a step. Are you kidding me? I knew enough that I needed to move her back over. When she stepped on her outside right foot, I gave her a little push with my hip and moved her back over. She dropped her shoulder and pushed me again, so I pushed her back. I was pissed. It didn't matter that she was a thousand pounds and could squish me like a bug. She tapped into a place that was still raw. I've never backed down from anyone or anything. We continued our football game around the arena until Kathryn finally intervened. We all switched horses.

The other horses were perfect. They walked beside me with heads down, and the testing was minimal. I looked around the arena and noticed that Maggie was being nice and sweet with everyone else.

At the end of the session, during our debriefing, Kathryn asked that we write down which horse we felt the most connected to and which we felt detached from. Frustrated, I wrote that I felt the most detached from Maggie. It was odd to hear others in the group name her as the horse they felt the most attached to. Our bonding experience would have to wait for another day, and, of course, I felt it was her fault. Everyone kept telling me that horses have memories like those of elephants. If that was true, why did she keep doing the same damn things after we had just resolved them the day before? Didn't she know that it made me angry when she challenged me all the time?

Over the next couple of days, I learned that less was more with my mare. The more aggressive I became, the more resistant and braced she became. I needed to quit taking it so personally. But so much of what I had been through over the last several years *felt* personal. Maggie's "job" was to challenge me and test me to see if I was worth following. And every time, I would over-react. Each time I overreacted, I solidified in her mind that I couldn't keep a level head and be her leader.

This is a pattern that has played out repeatedly throughout my lifetime. A teacher, a colleague, a dirt bag on the street or even my detachment commander would push and challenge me, and I would react. I was always up for a good fight. This exercise pointed out a behavioural cycle that I hadn't realized I was in. But that's what working with horses can do. It reveals patterns and opens up the opportunity for real change.

CHAPTER EIGHT

A Call for Change

Shortly after the Canadian Human Rights Commission settlement had been reached, in December 2008, I received a call from a then unfamiliar return-to-work coordinator. Sergeant Ron Campbell (his title at the time) asked me if we could meet. I had known this was coming, and I had in some ways been dreading this moment. I agreed to see him. My intention had always been to return to work after the complaint process had concluded. I assumed this meeting was to discuss next steps.

The two of us met at a café near my house and sat down at one of the tables. Even though things had been wrapped up and I had come to terms with the results, I was a little standoffish. I had committed to going through the back-to-work process, but my previous experiences kept me from being optimistic. Ron introduced himself, engaged in a little light chat, and then he dropped the bomb.

"On behalf of the organization, I would like to apologize to you for the way that you have been treated." He went on to say that the organization has a lot to learn about how to treat its employees. As I looked into his eyes and watched him deliver an apology that I had long since given up waiting for (having been resigned to the fact that it was never going to happen), I felt his genuineness. With that apology, one part of my ordeal was truly and finally over.

Ron asked me why, after everything I had been through, I wanted to go back to work for the RCMP. In 2004, I had voluntarily but reluctantly handed in my firearm, spare magazines, baton and pepper spray. Those were dark days for me. But I had done what I was supposed to do. My medical leave was granted because I was not well. It was my duty and responsibility to both my family and my employer to return to a state of health and wellness. Now that I was in a good place physically, mentally and emotionally, I felt strongly that I needed to play a role in helping other members who were in that same position.

So when Ron asked me why I wanted to come back, I simply replied, "Because I'm not done yet."

Ron Campbell understands psychological trauma better than most. On February 28, 2004, his life took a dramatic turn when an armed and mentally ill man barricaded himself in a house near the town of Spruce Grove, west of Edmonton. The man was schizophrenic, he was distraught, he had stopped taking his medication and he was drinking alcohol. He was hearing voices, his wife had told police before fleeing the house, and the voices were telling him to kill.

A crisis negotiator, Ron was called to the scene to try to

get through to the man, but that attempt failed, and when the deranged man tried to drive off in his truck, the decision was made by those in charge to ram the vehicle with an RCMP truck. In a subsequent exchange of gunfire, both the man and one officer—a dog handler and a longtime friend of Ron's—were killed.

"Thus began a downward spiral," Ron told me. "My past bubbled up, including other critical issues from twenty-two years ago. Today, I still live with post-traumatic stress disorder and major depressive disorder."

It took many years of therapy and experimentation to get the right combination of drugs to allow him to function and to beat back the anger, guilt, depression, insomnia and suicidal thoughts that tormented him. For almost a year, he tried to cover up his symptoms, until a female colleague called him out and, in his words, "busted me." Two simple questions was all it took.

"How are you doing?" she asked him.

"Fine," claimed Ron.

"No, how are you *really* doing?" she persisted, and then the truth spilled out. The daily thoughts of ending his own life. His normally chatty self gone silent. Troubles at home, with Ron pleading with his wife to leave him so he could be alone in his misery. His self-blame for the tragedy and inability to forgive himself.

Ron now works in human resources as a return-to-work coordinator for the RCMP. He still sees a counsellor, and he still takes medication and likely will for the rest of his life, but he feels better now than he has at any point in the past nine years. Ron has also become well-known as a public speaker. His topic? The damage done to police officers by police work.

What makes Ron Campbell special is that he can put on that serge uniform and talk—openly, candidly, freely—about the mental anguish that indisputably and invariably comes with police work. He has spoken on this subject all over North America and even Australia. I respect him, because he's not about choosing sides. It is automatically assumed within the force that if you criticize the organization that you don't support the organization. Nothing could be further from the truth. The goal of talking about the shortfalls of the RCMP is not to break the force down, but to improve it. We want it to be the organization it can and needs to be.

Ron laments that there is still some ignorance around psychological stress injuries. The injured continue to be seen as weak, when, in fact, depression, anxiety, compassion fatigue and PTSD are all normal, human responses to what Dr. Jeff Morley calls "prolonged exposure to unfixable suffering." Jeff is a registered psychologist and a veteran of the RCMP.

"Here's the crime," Ron says. "We"—and here he means the RCMP—"do nothing for prevention. I co-wrote the new course training standard for the crisis negotiation program used by the Canadian Police College, and I insisted there be a piece on self-care. People commit suicide right in front of you or on the phone. This is really hard. But the RCMP has no peer support program. Every other large police force in the country—Peel, Calgary, Edmonton, Vancouver—has full-time coordinators who connect officers who have been traumatized with others who have experience dealing with it."

Ron believes he has the support of high-ranking RCMP officers at the assistant commissioner level. But not, sadly, of the decision-makers. They don't seem to care about the attrition, he says. "Out with the old, in with the new."

In the end, Ron takes a positive view, but he does not hide his disappointment. "I am discouraged and disillusioned," he told me. "I don't see the appropriate leadership right now. But here's why I'm optimistic. We boomers are part of the problem. Sixty-six percent of our members have less than ten years' service. They are different. They want a better work–life balance, they're more inclined to seek help when they need it. There are some very good people out there, some very good detachment commanders. That's where the hope lies."

Can the RCMP change? Can law enforcement culture change? My initial response is no and no. In order for real change to happen, first, there must be acknowledgment that change is needed. Second, leaders need to walk their talk. And third, members need to be supported by consistent and compassionate leadership.

I believe this is why so many people find comfort in working with horses. The horses respond in the moment about how they are feeling. Their communication and intent are honest, clear (if you know what you're looking at) and immediate. And any adjustments—good or bad—I make to change the situation are acknowledged by the horse almost instantaneously. All the horse wants from me is for me to be a leader who can be respected and trusted, so the horse feels safe and secure enough to say yes when I ask her to do something that normally she may not want to do. In the presence of authentic leadership, a prey animal gives itself over to you, a predator, and thanks you in the process. In doing so, the horse puts itself completely in your hands.

A horse's number one priority twenty-four hours a day is

safety, but if you can prove that you are a worthy leader, the horse can rest and not worry during its time with you. The horse's mind and body can relax; the horse can and will literally exhale. That kind of communication and relationship just doesn't happen between members in the RCMP.

———

In the spring of 2013, RCMP Commissioner Bob Paulson gave a talk at headquarters in Edmonton. In an off-the-cuff speech that was posted as an audio clip on an RCMP watchdog site and also posted on the site of the Mounted Police Professional Association, he whistled and made a circular motion with his index finger at his head while speaking about PTSD. I'm not sure how you would interpret that gesture, but I would call it profoundly disrespectful of others' suffering.

In his remarks, Paulson suggested that the diagnosis of PTSD was not well understood and may be overused—a clear reference to malingerers—while at the same time he said that if members got sick, even psychologically, the RCMP would take care of them. I found that hard to stomach. The commissioner later issued a public apology for having been perceived to make light of psychological-related issues by using the sound and gesture, insisting that the force takes the issue of PTSD very seriously. His words felt hollow, and he did little to open the door for those who are suffering from operational stress injuries.

I am not broken; nor are all the other members who have psychological injuries. The system is broken. And although it was never my intention to "expose" the RCMP for all its faults, I feel a responsibility to tell the public that there are members reaching out for help, and it is easy for them to feel that nobody is listening.

When help isn't available, bad decisions and bad behaviour by RCMP officers can result. This is what makes the headlines, usually with a reference to "rogue Mounties."

The members most at risk of losing their jobs—not through dismissal, but through medical discharge—are those who suffer from psychological issues as a result of the job and who are no longer able to function in their regular duties.

The new generation of RCMP officers realizes on some level that they need help, but too many of the older generation still think *I never had help, so why should they need help?* The broken are pushed out the back door and fresh new faces eagerly walk through the front door, with no clue what lies in store for them.

I believe that in order for any real change to happen in the RCMP, a leader must be nominated and then chosen by the members who put their lives on the line every day. The commissioner's job should be a position elected by the uniformed membership, not hand-picked by the government in power. The commissioner should be completely autonomous of the government and have the ability to disagree and, when it's in the best interest of the membership, say no. An elected leader would give the members a revitalized sense of hope, because right now for many, "hope" is just another four-letter word. The other position within the organization that should be nomination- and election-based is the Chief Human Resource Officer (CHRO). Allowing the members to pick their leaders in these key positions would have a major impact in how the members feel about themselves and their organization.

I asked Jeff for his thoughts on leadership in the force. He made the point that the RCMP is generally pretty good at police work. Rarely do police leaders get into trouble over operational incompetence. How they treat people is the problem. Good leaders must show people competence as well as operational competence. Specifically, the realm of emotional intelligence is where leaders either crash and burn, or excel. Emotional intelligence is not soft and gooey. It is about the ability to be mindful and to regulate one's own emotions and reactions, and to recognize and work effectively with other people's emotions. "Not unlike equine therapy," he added.

"The importance of compassion cannot be overstated," Jeff continued. "Psychologist Dr. Daniel Goleman, who wrote a book on emotional intelligence, says that compassion is the prime inhibitor of human cruelty. This includes excessive force on the street, or in the office. When police leaders shame, embarrass, harass or attack an employee, it shows a lack of compassion, and basic human respect."

But in order for the RCMP to change, a good leader alone will not be sufficient. The members must realize that the organization is made up of individuals. It is the responsibility, the duty, of the members to hold themselves to the high standard they had when they entered the force. I've worked with dozens of good officers, and yet they often can't seem to overcome the nastiness of the world.

What the organization needs more than anything are heroes, members who are willing to stand up for the masses, regardless of rank and despite the consequences. Heroes are not to be confused with martyrs. It should not be required that someone sacrifice his or her career in order to initiate and support change.

The key is to get the uniformed members involved in the process of change and actually ask them what they think and what they need. There is a huge disconnect between management in the RCMP and the frontline members. One cannot succeed without the other, and each needs to see the other as important.

––––––––––

How can RCMP officers effectively go into communities and be the examples of honesty, integrity and morality, knowing that the organization they work for is scrambling to find its own honesty, integrity and morality? That's the disconnect; that's the underlying frustration. The members who know better are caught between knowing the truth and upholding the force's image within the community.

The organization is a microcosm of the real world. And that includes people who are simply jumping on the bandwagon to bring down the RCMP. This, too, is reality: some people tell the truth, some lie, some take advantage. People are people.

The RCMP wants its members and the public to believe that we in the RCMP are a better, superior group of people. The public wants and needs to believe it, because we all need to believe that those sworn to protect and serve are doing so from a higher standard of morality. The members need to believe it because it's our lifeline to sanity. If we don't believe we have a higher standard, then why not take the money from a drug raid? Why not punch the drunk in the face when he calls you names? We have to tell ourselves that we're better than that, knowing in our hearts that we're just people too. We make mistakes just like everyone else. We lie about our mistakes, or do our best to put our misdeeds or bad judgments into a context that diminishes them. We are good people (most of us), but everyone has that touch of darkness in them. All human beings, under the right circumstances, can, in the moment, choose to do something they wouldn't normally do.

If the RCMP's goal is to recruit and pick the best of the best, then either the recruitment process is failing or the organization is failing its members after the fact.

What about malingerers—members of the force working the system to their advantage? Ron and Jeff agree that "5 percent tops" are trying to duck duty. The overwhelming peer pressure is the other way—to ignore symptoms, to come back to work before you're ready, to "suck it up"—because every day off duty sick inflicts a punishment on your co-workers. In your absence, they have to work harder and longer.

It is certainly true that prolonged absences in the workplace negatively impact everyone. As with maternity leaves, there is nothing in place that allows the organization to temporarily fill these positions, so the members who are still working are forced to pick up the slack. The officer feels guilty for being off sick, and there is a significant amount of internal and external pressure for that officer to return to work—well or not. The officers left behind eventually feel anger and frustration at their increase in workload.

Some detachment commanders address too often this unhealthy dynamic. They get their own hands and boots dirty by taking simple calls, by taking a night shift or two to cover. They step up and help out. But detachment commanders can to often encourage and foster the resentment. Increased pressure, the thinking must go, will force members back to work or force them out altogether.

The ties to the RCMP family are conditional. You are part of the family as long as you stay healthy (or do what it takes to *appear* healthy), put your work before everything and everyone else and do as you're told. Shared experience of trauma can bring officers together, but there's a false sense of connection there. Members of the RCMP feel this most acutely when they retire from the force and the building entry codes are changed the second they leave their old detachments. When you leave the force, you leave "the club."

Members are driven by fear. Not so far back in our minds is the intense desire to make it through the shift and go home at the end of the day or night. We have families—loved ones depending on us to walk through our front doors eight, ten or twelve hours after we left. Nobody wants to get hurt or killed. The drive to survive is human nature, which pushes us into an even higher level of alertness and hypersensitivity. We observe on some level of consciousness how others are treated when they are injured. And we know we don't want to be one of them. We are conditioned to believe that only the weak are susceptible to injury and the strong suck it up. It is a community based on fear and shame.

There is much debate about the militarization of police forces in Canada and the United States. Police officers increasingly feel the need to protect themselves. If I were still on the frontline, I would view the extra armour, the higher-powered firearms and the armoured vehicles as an extra layer of protection. Now, I see them from a slightly different perspective. I still view them as a way for police officers to protect themselves, but they are also an added boundary between the police and the public. It adds to the division, increasing the space between "Us" and "Them."

Jeff has exhaustively examined the available research. He knows, for example, that police officers generally don't trust other people. The studies say that 92 percent of cops are suspicious, but from all his presentations across the country, he thinks that number is actually low. Police officers are at greater risk for depression (21 percent suffer from it, as compared to 4 percent in the general population). About 11 percent of police officers report suicidal thoughts as a result of their work. Seven to 9 percent suffer from PTSD, and 33 percent suffer from partial PTSD. Some 81 percent develop new prejudices on the job, and 82 percent believe the world is unsafe.

Much of the research, Jeff says, is dated, and most of it is from the United States. Anyone curious to know the rates of psychological distress in RCMP officers can only guess, because no research is being done. Health records systems, says Jeff, are outdated and inadequate to provide accurate statistics. And even these records would not be reliable because untold numbers of RCMP members surely suffer in silence, are afraid to speak up or seek out care and pay for it privately so the RCMP does not know about it.

In a recent interview on the Global Television program *16x9*, Assistant Commissioner Gilles Moreau acknowledged that cultural barriers around mental health issues still exist within the RCMP and that "we need to change that, as it's not acceptable." While a new mental health strategy has been launched within the RCMP, when asked by the *16x9* journalist if the RCMP should be taking a serious look at whether what they are doing is working, Moreau answered, "We could, yes. Are we doing that right now? No. We are a policing organization and we have to focus our resources toward that."

I met Melanie while playing soccer in 2012. Even though we played on the same team and were told by others on the team that we were both members of the RCMP, we never talked about our common employment. I would go so far as to say that we politely avoided each other. We shared the same dressing room, played on the same field, and sat around the same table after the games for more than six months, but never once talked about anything other than soccer. Each of us was afraid of being judged by the other. As Mel told me not too long ago, "Not only the fear of being judged but the shame associated."

Shame. I still feel shame. I sometimes still feel the shame of taking medical leaves, the shame of freezing on the bridge that day and the shame of losing my compassion for others and myself. An organization that you had put on such a high pedestal tells you that you're weak, and you start to believe it. Leaving a club you once admired inevitably feels like failure.

It took several months before Melanie and I talked about our experiences in the RCMP. She described to me her surprise and her frustration: "My own people were bullying and harassing me, and in numerous ways."

In January 2013, she left the force and began her new job (which she loves) at the Alberta Human Rights Commission. Meanwhile, she has launched three separate complaints with the Canadian Human Rights Commission over lost wages, pension and promotions. Not lost on Melanie is the irony of going from the RCMP, where she says her human rights were abused, to an outfit where human rights is the focus.

"I'm very proud of the work I did with the RCMP," Melanie says. "I held myself to a high standard, and I'm glad I had the opportunity to serve my country. I loved my job so much, but it's always a struggle to be a woman in the RCMP. And is there any more stressful job? No. Had there been an apology, that would have made a huge difference. There was no one in my camp. I waited a full year for someone to do the right thing."

———

By June 2013, I had not seen my old partner Sue in a long time. I called her and asked if she had time to meet for lunch somewhere close to where she now lived, about three hours south of Edmonton. I was putting this part of my memoir together, and I wanted to ask her some questions. More important, I had a need to see an old friend. Even though we're back in the same province, our in-person visits are few and far between. I didn't know what to expect. I knew from phone calls and emails that her health had declined perilously in recent years. I was aware that she struggles with fibromyalgia and chronic migraines, that she has PTSD, that she sees a chiropractor and physiotherapist just about every day to deal with her various mangled parts (knees, neck, back and a twice-fractured hand). I knew, too, that she continued to battle the RCMP over the question of compensation and medical benefits.

Sue is what I would have become had I stayed in the force. She's a fighter, and she's mightily attached to the idea of being a Mountie. But being a Mountie sucked the life right out of her. Right now, good health and pain-free days seem a long way off and may not be attainable at all. I wanted Sue to have a place in this book as a way of remembering her and all that she did for me. Perhaps I can—in this testimonial about her—honour her in a way that the RCMP never could, even had it tried to.

I cannot think of Sue without smiling. Truly, she made me laugh when we worked together, and she still makes me laugh today. She was a gutsy, dedicated cop, and it distresses me to see her being treated without compassion by the organization to which she dedicated the better part of her life.

Sue is also symbolic of all members of the RCMP. What's that saying? All gave some and some gave all? Sue gave all. She gave up having a family, and she gave up balance in her life between work and play. Her dedication and commitment, the way she cared for both the public and her fellow officers, were remarkable.

Sue was a true "high flyer"—that's cop parlance for an officer who has a knack for catching bad guys and has the knowledge and skills to make her the best at what she does. After more than twenty-five years of service (including a wild nine-month stint as a United Nations police officer during a tumultuous time in East Timor in 2002 and 2003), Sue's body is a mess. She's depleted on every level.

As we talked, I realized not much had changed in the time we hadn't seen each other. Quick, and at times hysterically funny, capable and smart, and confident to the point of cockiness, Sue is that crackerjack cop you'd want as your co-worker. In some ways, she has not changed at all since the days when she was my mentor. Burly, round-shouldered and, I knew from having worked out with her in the gym, immensely strong in her prime. Fearless, sarcastic, sharp-tongued, sassy. Not a woman to tangle with. Her work had clearly taken its toll on her, but it had also given her enough characters, stories and vignettes to create an original play.

Here, for example, are a few definitions in the Sue dictionary:

White shirts. Normally this refers to RCMP brass, but Sue views it as "the first level of incompetence."

Commendation. The framed medal she has on her wall at home for disarming a knife-wielding assailant in the bar of the Oxford Brooks Hotel (a.k.a. "The Zoo") in Brooks, Alberta, in 1990. As Sue puts it, the medal was "for not shooting someone I should have shot."

Widow-makers. The holsters she used in those days, with the snaps that didn't work so the gun would sometimes fall right through the holster and onto the floor.

Top-of-the-line equipment. See above.

Like a blind man put it together. The RCMP uniform she wore in those days, with the famously mismatched blue pants and brown shirt.

It's terminal. When told that Jeff had likened the RCMP as an organization to a "treatment-resistant" patient, Sue offered another, grimmer prognosis.

Two out of nine. The number of detachments, in Sue's eyes, that met her standard.

Seven out of thirty. The number of female cops, in Sue's eyes, who met her standard.

Boo-Boo and Numpkey. Her nicknames for two particularly inept members who will get starring roles should Sue ever take her show on the road.

———

There is a part of Sue that remains loyal to the force and proud to have worn that uniform. Like me, she graduated from Depot all gung-ho and ready to get the bad guys. The fact that her commendation is on her wall at home and not stuck at the back of a sock drawer speaks to that old pride in a job well done. When Sue had your back, you were truly covered.

"I think we did walk that middle road, you and I," she told me. "We hugged people. Stuff with kids and abused women. Lots of houses, I knew I was coming back. That's why we have all this shit." Sue meant the long-term psychological damage done. "You can't do the job without an impact."

———

The incident in the bar, the incident that earned Sue a commendation, makes for a good story. But events like this take a toll.

She describes entering adjoining bars in that hotel we called The Zoo, for all the trouble that went down there. The call had come in: a man in one of the bars had been using a butcher knife to slice people, and he had locked one barmaid in the cooler. Accompanied by a smaller, less assertive female RCMP officer, Sue now faced the man. He was big, and he was drunk, but not nearly drunk enough for Sue's liking, and he casually held the pay phone receiver in one hand and the knife in the other.

"The cops are here," Sue heard him to say into the phone. "I have to kill them now."

Then he hung up. "I'm going to kill you," he said. Then he lunged at her, and she leapt back. Only when the man made a move toward her partner did Sue pull out her gun, but still she was reluctant to use it because of the crowd that now surrounded them. As for her partner's gun? It was lying on the street outside the hotel. Her holster had not properly snapped. Widow-maker indeed. The missing revolver would have been a terribly black and salient detail had things really gone south in that bar.

In the end, Sue cracked the man across the wrist with her oversized flashlight, got him down to the floor and handcuffed him. No one killed. No one hurt. No shots fired. The Mountie got her man, who got thirty days in jail—served on weekends.

Two years in Brooks, Sue says, was like ten years in real time. Shootings, robberies, stabbings. And gender was always an issue. She resented the sexist remarks of superiors ("bullet-proof breasts"); she resented the looks she got on the street (looks reserved for female officers). "I did not," she says resentfully, "take the *female* version of the oath when I joined the RCMP."

Sue and I hugged and bade farewell. She got into her truck, a big blue number with double wheels over the rear axle. I had to smile to myself, watching her climb into this massive piece of machinery. It would certainly afford her a sense of safety, but it also struck me that this vehicle was very much like Sue: a force to be reckoned with.

As we drove off in our separate directions, I wondered when I would see her again. I met Sue more than seventeen years ago in the office of my first detachment. Since then she's been my trainer, my mentor, my maid of honour and my one and only sister-friend. When I see her or hear her voice, I experience waves of emotion. I'm grateful that she is close enough to visit. But I'm angry that she experiences such intense pain as a result of her physical injuries and her other, more intimate injuries—which are equally debilitating. I feel more anger at the organization she has sacrificed herself to. Her body said no a long time ago, but she pushed on.

At times I have felt immense guilt. Sue never stopped until her body forced her to, but I did. I was spared a similar fate by some freak accident and an unwillingness to shove the knowledge of my injury under the proverbial carpet. If anyone deserves to be healthy and happy, it's Sue. And yet, after everything I've learned about operational stress injuries and everything I've done—I can't find a way to take my dear friend's pain away.

There was a time when I wondered if our friendship would withstand the fact that I was no longer a police officer on the street. Many members have come and gone from my life, and I've managed to stay in touch with only a handful. The key has always been that we have more in common than just the RCMP. I trusted Sue with my life in many situations, and she trusted me. It was the beginning of a truly unique and special bond that few people will probably ever experience. Our friendship is entrenched in that foundation, but the roots run much deeper than that.

Harassment and failed leadership in the RCMP is not exclusively a gender issue; it's a *cultural* one. Getting stuck in the male versus female dynamics of harassment is a way for the RCMP to deflect the core issue. What is truly lacking is compassionate leadership.

During the summer of 2014, the media reported that there had been twenty-three first responder suicides in the previous six months. And just a short period of time after that report, another tragic incident came to light when an RCMP member took his life after a long battle with PTSD.

After I heard the news about the number of suicides that had occurred across Canada, I felt a sense of panic. The big picture of those tragedies felt overwhelming. When I say that word, it doesn't quite fit. People often feel a sense of being overwhelmed; it's a normal way of life for many. We feel overwhelmed with work, life and the human condition in general. Sometimes when I think back to my darkest days, it seems like such a huge leap from how I felt then to how I feel now. But other times it feels like it's just across the road. I understand how and why people get to that point. *Overwhelmed* isn't the right word. What I felt was anger. Yet when I look past that, what I truly felt was immense sadness.

There are lots of individuals and groups who have done a great job of raising awareness about these types of injuries—but now what? People still feel like they have nowhere to go, no one to turn to. The next step is to increase the awareness and accessibility of the programs and services available. Unfortunately, the bottom line is always funding, or lack thereof.

CHAPTER NINE

Good Medicine

My psychologist once described me as a "justice seeker." My belief in right and wrong is deep-seated. I find comfort in order and fairness. This is my thinking: Do the right thing, and you will be rewarded; do the wrong thing, and life should bite you. I took seriously my oath to become a police officer, and I did my best to honour the uniform I wore. I am one to start off with kindness, but if that kindness is not reciprocated, then things can change in an instant, and I won't quit until I win. The point of going through all my grievances and harassment complaints was to get someone within the RCMP to step up and say, "What happened to you is not acceptable." I was eagerly waiting for an intervention at the highest level, someone to bring order to my chaos.

There were times when I saw a police car drive by and felt a deep sense of sadness and shame because I couldn't be that person driving that police car anymore. My daughter Skylar, then five, was old enough to understand what a police officer was, and she would ask me why I never wore my uniform. I was still with the force then, but non-operational. Skylar cried when I told her I wouldn't ever be able to give her a ride in a cruiser. Seeing my uniforms hanging in a downstairs closet just wasn't the same as having her police officer mom come to her kindergarten class in full uniform or watching me in red serge march in a parade.

That identity continued to drift, and that same year, I began to see beyond the small, intense world that I had created for myself. It was time to discover the person standing behind that glorious red uniform.

I had, for the most part, accepted my hearing loss, and I had accepted that I would never work on the street as a police officer again. I had walked that route and come to a dead end. Part of me, a small part of me, wanted to stay on it, even if it wasn't going anywhere—simply because it was familiar.

But another part of me, the greater part, was now ready to try a new path. What was required, and what horses provide, is a new perspective. It took only a tiny shift in my way of thinking to open up a new world. Horses allowed me to see things differently, and working with them inspired a change in my life that I would have never thought possible.

———

In February 2010, when I was ten months into what would be my final posting with the RCMP (working in the commercial crime unit in Edmonton), I made a trip out to Riversong Ranch to discuss what I called at the time the War Horse Project. I was handling my depression pretty well, I thought, and I felt like I was in a good space. I was working three days a week at the detachment and devoting a great deal of time and energy to this fledgling idea of working with horses to begin addressing work-induced trauma.

The idea was to bring together individuals from different policing organizations to discuss the issue of operational stress injuries. Post-traumatic stress disorder (PTSD) and other related conditions are not unique to the RCMP. If I could reach out to like-minded people within other policing organizations and bring them together, real progress could be made.

Meanwhile, I was experiencing for myself the silence and isolation that many RCMP officers can expect when they return to work after an occupational stress injury. I had expected the cold shoulder, and I very much kept to myself. Most members are not supportive of off-duty sick leaves, in no small part because the current system doesn't allow for replacements when fellow officers can't work.

After coming back to work, I felt a general tension between the other members and myself, and were it not for my staff sergeant, my situation would have been much worse. In a typical detachment, you have three groups: the active duty officers, the ones who are or were off duty sick, and a small group in the middle who are active duty officers who feel some compassion for their fellow officers. I wanted the walls to come down. I wanted some sort of conversation among us to begin, but I had no idea what shape that might take. But I knew this much: I wasn't ready to talk about this subject in my own office. I thought I'd be more comfortable talking to strangers—at the symposium that was starting to take shape.

Chris and Kathryn generously offered to donate Riversong Ranch and their time to the event. We picked a date in September of that year. The idea of working *with* people, instead of fighting every step of the way, was enticing. I had spent so much time swimming against the current. I looked forward to the possibility of going with the flow for a change.

I immediately started calling municipal police forces in the province. The first step was to find out what programs various organizations already had in place and whether or not they were interested in sharing their information. The larger municipal police forces had peer-support coordinators or Critical Incident Stress Management (CISM) members who were involved in debriefing their fellow officers after a major incident. I was surprised and heartened by the positive response. They were ready and willing to share their information and believed there would be great value in coming together to discuss an issue that affects so many.

I began stepping out of the policing world and contacting other groups—the Canadian armed forces, ambulance workers, firefighters, corrections officers, sheriffs and fish and wildlife officers. In many instances, we respond to the same kinds of events. And although we may experience trauma in different ways (because our roles are different), the trauma manifests itself similarly. PTSD, depression and addictions affect more than just police officers.

As I've described, however, police officers have a tendency to isolate themselves. We feel like no one understands what we go through, that we have nowhere to turn, and our support system is often limited. We largely rely on each other, and yet we are arguably the most judgmental group of people on the face of the earth. And while we rely on each other and share with each other, we often do so in dysfunctional ways. It was time to make our support system bigger.

In time, one person led me to another, who led me to another. A wonderful woman from Alberta Health Services, Careen Condrotte, offered to help me organize the symposium and to nail down exactly what I was trying to accomplish. I had no experience in organizing such a gathering. I had a vision and an idea of what I wanted it to look like, but her experience in coordinating these types of events was pivotal in transitioning the idea into something real. I am grateful that she jumped on board.

I contacted Jeff Morley—I knew him then only by reputation; we hadn't yet met—and invited him to the symposium. A registered psychologist and veteran of the force, he, too, was very supportive and made a commitment to attend. I had no idea that making that one phone call would initiate the relationship that I now have with Jeff. He would become a friend, a mentor and a huge supporter of my efforts and of me. The same can be said of Ron Campbell, who likewise accepted the invitation to come, and supported both me and the symposium. I can't possibly express how much it meant to me to have the backing of two members of the RCMP who were in management positions. I felt as though I had found a small pocket of people who were on the same page, and it was refreshing. Discovering members who believed in helping other members gave me a sense of hope, something I hadn't had in a long time.

I was amazed at the group of people who came together for that first symposium, but I was also nervous and unsure. While we had the same outlook, we all seemed to be so consumed with what we were working on individually that I wasn't convinced all these type A personalities could work together. Still, the range of those attending was remarkable: there were first responders, including some with PTSD, of course, but also individuals advocating for such people, a clinical psychologist, and two officers from the Peel Regional Police Force in Ontario.

I had brought all these people together to share information about occupational stress injuries, but I really wanted so much more than that. That first year I wanted everyone who came to make a presentation on what their own organizations were doing, or not doing, about work-induced trauma. Some organizations, we discovered, didn't want to address the issue, while others were keen to get as much information as they could. My overall impression was that very little was being done to prevent or address the problem. And my prime goal was to get all these groups talking to one another. What challenges did we have in common? What services were actually working, and which were not? Were there some best practices out there that we could take back to our workplaces? How does trauma impact frontline service providers—and their families?

I scheduled the agenda to allow for Chris to start the day with a demonstration with a horse in the round pen. I wanted those at the symposium to experience the way horses can get people to see with new perspective.

Almost everyone who came to that first symposium at Riversong Ranch—and almost everyone since—remarked on the peace of the place. Kathryn once told me, "This place has been my good medicine, and I hope it can be that for you too."

And it has been. Every time I go to Riversong, I feel this soul-soothing sense of peace. Experience after experience at Riversong left me wondering—not necessarily believing—that maybe there was more order than chaos to this world. I was so angry for so long. I am first and foremost a cynic. If I didn't see it or experience it, it didn't happen and it's not possible. The more time I spent at Riversong and with the horses, the more things started to happen to make me feel like I was part of something bigger than myself.

It felt good to rub shoulders with people who had direct experience of occupational stress: nurses, ambulance workers, firefighters, soldiers, police officers, border guards, social workers. We knew more than a little about PTSD or anxiety or depression or addiction or anger management issues—and some of us had experienced all of them.

During lunch breaks, we would stand by the paddocks, or sit in lawn chairs and just observe the horses grazing. How can you *not* watch a horse grazing? There is a great deal of scientific evidence to show that grooming a horse or even watching a goldfish swim around an aquarium can lower blood pressure and induce calm.

No sounds of traffic. No phones ringing. No deadlines. I was even out of wireless range, so my communications devices had gone silent.

All of us at that first symposium could feel ourselves decompress, the quiet of the place settling over us. Seeing the horses, working with them, all worked a little magic on us.

———

The Second Annual War Horse Symposium took place in September 2011. Careen again helped me organize. The number of participants doubled from the first year and included even more groups from one end of the country to the other—including a former police officer from Halifax who told a harrowing tale of his alcohol addiction and a suicide attempt before he emerged from the darkness to coordinate a peer-support program for first responders and their families. Chris and Kathryn again donated their time, and once again opened the doors to their beautiful property. I was more confident that second year, more certain that working with horses was a help to me in my struggles and more convinced that horses could help open the door to healing for others.

At that second symposium, I talked about the concept of "mine is bigger than yours." First responders sometimes get caught fighting about who is the most damaged group and become stuck there. Police officers have more issues than firefighters and firefighters have it much worse than social workers, and on and on. We don't need this hierarchy of who is the most broken. If we could agree to acknowledge that we *all* experience trauma, and not get stuck on what roles we play, we could then move on to the part where we could actually figure out what we are going to do about it.

Another block standing in the way of progress is our "us versus them" mentality. Fighting becomes comfortable and familiar. As police officers, we often fight civilians, our own organization, each other—and we become addicted to the fight. At one point, I was fighting everyone. I wanted and needed the fight. But if we can focus on our similarities and on our wellness, we will be so much stronger.

Isolation is a major factor in our inability to move forward.

We all believe that we're the only ones feeling a certain way or going through whatever it is we're going through. I thought I could handle my depression by myself, and that if I couldn't handle it, I was even weaker than I had thought. We all too often suffer in silence. The only person in my life I was not fighting with was my husband, an amazing and compassionate man. From him, I simply withdrew. Small wonder that relationships fall apart under the strain of these types of injuries.

The stigma of PTSD or depression or addiction is there because we allow it to exist. At some level, we succumb to the belief that we don't deserve any better. I know that I am not alone. And I want others to know that they are not alone either. There is someone out there experiencing the same thoughts and feelings as you are and they need you as much as you need them. The purpose of both the symposium and the foundation is to make our worlds and our support systems bigger. We must stand together if we are ever to truly heal our wounds.

———————

By degrees I left the RCMP.

On April 24, 2013, I handed in my badge. And on May 1, my last day, I gave up my soft body armour, my gun belt, my pass to the Division headquarters and my Blackberry. I still have my serge uniform, the hat, the boots—technically, I am allowed to wear them to the funerals of former colleagues, though I doubt I ever will.

Entering the RCMP's K headquarters on that final day gave me a bittersweet feeling. I was leaving behind a big part of my life. I had grown up in that organization. I was grateful for my experiences, good and bad, for they shaped who I am. I wanted to allow myself that, to feel the sense of loss.

That day, as it turned out, the staff sergeant who accepted my last pieces of who I once was, was dealing with the death of a friend, a civilian employee of the RCMP who had served overseas where he was exposed to a chemical that killed him. I had gone into his office prepared to be consoled in some way, but my staff sergeant was the one in need of consoling. So there was no pity party. Losing one's career was nothing compared to losing one's life. At the time I didn't welcome the perspective on this ending to a very long and hard-fought chapter of my life, but looking back I can see that it gave me a much-needed perspective.

As I left K Division headquarters in Edmonton that day, I also felt regret. I thought I had prepared myself for this day, had imagined myself doing cartwheels across the parking lot. I certainly felt a sense of freedom. I walked away knowing that I had done everything I could to be a part of change within the organization, but it had become clear that the force and I were moving in very different directions. I wasn't angry anymore, but I still felt a deep sense of disappointment. My options were to risk being pulled back into a way of being and thinking that went against everything I had come to believe, or to take my experiences and move on. It was time to move on.

The nine years between handing in my gun and handing in my badge had been a roller coaster for me. I had gone from the detachment at Redwater to a medical leave to working with Project KARE, aimed at solving the murders of women in the Edmonton area. I needed and wanted a permanent "home"—not to be stuck somewhere doing what I perceived to be unfulfilling tasks, such as putting Crime Stoppers tips in numerical order. I needed meaningful work, something I could sink my teeth into. I didn't need any more time to think than I already had.

Then came another medical leave before landing work with ViCLAS—the Violent Crime Linkage System, aimed at tracking violent offenders. I loved this work, and I truly thought I had finally found an ideal spot within the RCMP. Home at last. I admired my supervisor, who, in turn, liked the work I was doing. But then he was transferred, and that was the end of that tenure for me. The new temporary member in charge informed me that my position was a pet project initiated entirely by the previous unit commander and that it was not supported beyond that. As the job had been created expressly for me and because its loss left me with few alternatives that were interesting to me, I felt as if I wasn't supported either.

Losing that job after only five months was the straw that broke the camel's back. There followed my maternity leave, a medical leave, and then four years working in the RCMP's commercial crime unit in Edmonton.

By leaving the RCMP, I knew one thing: I was getting my family back. I had missed so much, especially of my daughter Skylar's childhood. When I was in the throes of my battles with the force over my grievance, my hearing loss and my supervisor, I had nothing left for family. My marriage suffered (counselling saved the relationship), and though we never fought in front of Skylar and Kassidy, the former as a toddler had huge difficulty sleeping at night. Was there tension in the house? Absolutely. Did she pick up on it? Most likely.

When Kassidy was born, on October 4, 2006, naturally Jerry

and I had experienced the joy of her birth. But emotionally and physically, I was not at my best. Kassidy and Skylar were four years apart. We had wanted our children to be closer in age, but I kept postponing the thought of another child as I battled my hearing issue, depression and, of course, the RCMP. Kassidy was in utero when the job at ViCLAS went up in smoke, and I was once more back in work limbo.

Back then I was in survival mode—trying to save my career, myself, my marriage, and trying to be a new mother. It was all too much. And in the end, the hearing loss wasn't what caused me to finally quit the RCMP. How I felt treated by my own organization caused it all to come crashing down and it was time to pursue the work I found meaningful.

———

On August 23, 2013, I received by mail a Certificate of Service from the RCMP. Also in the mail was a form letter signed by the Prime Minister of Canada thanking me on behalf of the government and people of Canada for sixteen years of loyal service. There was a time in my career when I would have thrown both these pieces of paper in the trash. I would have viewed them as hollow words—reminders of the difficult times. Not because there weren't any good times, but because my mind often takes pleasure in focusing on the bad.

The truth is that during my policing career I saw things I wasn't prepared to see. I experienced events that were psychologically, emotionally and intellectually beyond any coping skills or strategies that I possessed. I also witnessed acts of great bravery and compassion, but my mind is so eager to forget those moments. Unfortunately, in the life of service it seems the more one cares, the more one suffers. If good people are destined to suffer because they care so much, then what's the point?

Maybe the point is not to see myself as broken, but to cherish myself as the person I've become—not in spite of, but because of, my experiences. What if trauma isn't meant as a time to suffer, but as an opportunity for transformation?

I have choices. The choice is to be bitter or better. I've done bitter, but better, quite frankly, is a lot more fun. So, although the certificate and the letter will probably not win a place on my living room wall, they won't be found in the trash either.

I'm proud to have served.

———

With every War Horse Symposium, I became more and more confident. With the passage of time, I could talk about things such as the end of my career in the force without feeling sad. Someone asked me while I was writing this book, "How do you feel?" I said, "I feel good," and I meant it. It may sound trivial for most, but it really was a milestone. For so long, I thought I would never feel joy again.

I felt some fear around this time, but it had more to do with household economics than with working in the RCMP. In the spring of 2013, Jerry quit his job too—and for reasons not unlike mine. He had been working as an inspector for the Alberta government, examining dangerous goods equipment and highway tanks to ensure they were suitable for transporting dangerous and toxic material—everything from oil to chemicals. But that job also required that he attend accident scenes, and one particularly gruesome event (a tractor trailer had caught fire and the driver was killed) traumatized him.

Now we both had PTSD. I had officially been diagnosed by a psychologist not long after leaving the force. Sadly, with his diagnosis Jerry felt he was not supported. He felt his bosses responded much as most RCMP bosses respond. "I'm fine; what's wrong with you?"

One good thing about my own PTSD was that I well knew what Jerry was going through, and I urged him to get help—which he did.

Jerry left his job and started up his own consulting business. So there we were, with Skylar and Kassidy still in primary school, and neither parent had a job. But I had huge confidence that Jerry would land on his feet, and more and more that looks to be the case. My hope is that the War Horse Symposiums will continue to grow and reach more and more people.

That possibility took another step forward just before the symposium in the fall of 2013, when the War Horse Foundation was granted charitable status.

CHAPTER TEN

Seeing the Light

I n 2013, after the second draft of this book was complete, I began to experience some changes in my sleep pattern. It's not unusual for me to go through periods of being unable to fall asleep or waking up and not being able to fall back to sleep. For the most part, I view it as a part of life—the consequence of long years of shiftwork.

During that time, I had also made the decision to go public with my story. Almost immediately, an opportunity arose. I heard about a roundtable that was to be held in Edmonton, the fourth of five such forums being held across the country to examine issues of harassment in the RCMP. The events were initiated by Toronto MP Judy Sgro and Senator Grant Mitchell of Alberta. I sent Ms. Sgro an email briefly explaining my story and adding that I would like to attend the forum. I received a note back from one of her assistants asking if I would be willing to talk to the media. They had encountered several RCMP members who had very compelling stories, but no one would actually talk on camera. Being in a position of having the freedom to speak with no consequences to my career, I said I would.

Shortly after the forum, a piece appeared in *The Huffington Post* under the title "How RCMP Harassment Ruined One Woman's Life." I was horrified. I had given *The Huffington Post* permission to use the email, but I had expected more. My life had not been ruined by harassment in the RCMP. It's so much easier to point out the negatives than to focus on the positives. My life now, the symposiums, the foundation—I had spoken during the roundtable about all of that. But none of it made it into the piece. It was my first lesson in politics.

A couple of months later, I was contacted by CTV News. They were doing a story about PTSD in the RCMP and wanted to know if I was interested in doing an interview. Again, several members were part of the piece, but nobody was willing to appear on camera. Later, I would learn that Jeff Morley was also part of the story.

The reporter came to my house and conducted a two-hour interview. During that interview, I was asked about some of my traumatic experiences. I told the story about being on the bridge and disclosed to him the nightmares that made me feel like I was losing my mind. I had told the story a few times before, and I believed the more I told it, the easier it would be—the less emotion it would stir. And yet, even this time, I was overcome.

I didn't understand. How could I still be reacting to an incident that happened more than ten years ago? I had made peace with it, had I not? I understood the fight, flight or freeze response, and how that splint-second reaction affects the brain and body. I understood and had moved on, so why did telling this story still elicit an emotional response? It made me angry and frustrated. I knew the reporter would use that piece for the televised interview—they wouldn't turn down that kind of drama.

The story aired, and I watched it alone in the basement while the rest of my family viewed it upstairs. Why? Several reasons. I am a complete introvert, and there is still a sense of shame about speaking publicly about something so private. I was embarrassed to be seen talking about such matters in front of my family and embarrassed that I had not contained my emotions during the interview.

I continued to hope the focus of the piece would be the symposium and the foundation, but inside I knew better. There I was on my big-screen television, tears in my eyes—vulnerable as vulnerable could be. I thought the piece was well done overall, but I was disappointed that not one word appeared about resources or programs available to help those who are struggling to deal with these types of injuries. The reporter told me that the six-minute piece was not long enough to include that information, but he did offer to attend the 2014 symposium and do a story dedicated to the solutions and not the problems. Unfortunately, the reporter didn't respond to my emails after the story aired and did not attend the symposium.

Shortly after the interview aired, I began to experience violent dreams. All that kept going through my head was, No, no, no. Anything but the nightmares. I was aware of my anxiety building, but the tools I had relied on before—such as meditation and exercise—were not providing any relief. The anxiety was a result of experiencing the nightmares, but also the shame of it all. This book was supposed to be about me coming out the other side, when clearly I had not—at least not yet. I told myself, I can't go through this again, especially not now.

The more I tried to suppress the anxiety, of course, the more I could feel my feet coming off the ground. For the first time in years, I was again living in fear. This time, at least I wasn't compelled to sleep with a firearm within arm's reach as I had done many years before.

I don't know exactly when I had started to feel compelled to sleep close to my gun. I would guess it was shortly after the bridge incident. This feeling carried through for years after we moved to Redwater.

When Skylar started walking, I had to move the firearm higher to keep it out of her reach. We purchased a firearms safe when she was a bit older. Not having the gun close in a drawer caused me some anxiety. I would rehearse every night in my head before I went to sleep how many steps it was to the door of the safe, depending on which side of the bed I rolled off. I would practise the code in my head and run through several different scenarios. Most of the scenarios involved someone breaking into the house and grabbing one of the girls.

This new fear—since the interview aired—was of another kind. Fear of losing control, fear of going back into the darkness and fear of being exposed as a fraud. I had learned enough over the past few years to know that I needed help, and the sooner, the better. I called my psychologist, who informed me that to have medical insurance coverage (now through Veterans Affairs Canada [VAC], because I was retired), I would have to obtain a doctor's referral. Just this one extra step caused me to pause. I had made the effort to reach out for help and now I was required to see my doctor and explain to him that I needed to see my psychologist. There was a nagging voice, quiet as it was, that said, *No way. They're making it too hard. There's no reason why I should have to get a note from some doctor who I haven't had the need to see in several years and explain to him why I need to see my psychologist. This is bullshit.*

Then another inner voice, surprisingly loud and strong, spoke up and said, *You know better.*

And I do. I put my ego and shame in my pocket and made my appointment with the doctor, and left with my referral note. I made my choice.

The initial sessions with my psychologist were for the assessment phase. I told her about the dreams and how the dreams triggered other behavioural cycles. Once I felt the fear, the next step was to push everyone away. I didn't want anyone to see what I was going through. An old pattern—withdrawal, isolation, irritability, quickness to anger—resurfaced. My first instinct is to withdraw. I feel very much like I need to handle the fear on my own. I had begun my process of shutting down, and I needed help to stop it.

After my second session, my psychologist asked me to make a chart and write out my fears. I went home and wrote the word *FEAR* in the middle of the paper and circled it. I made lines in every direction and got into the nitty-gritty. The first word I wrote down was *nightmares*. Something about the nightmares is particularly bothersome. Maybe I associate them with the first step of really feeling out of control. The word that followed was *depression*. My first round of major depression had left me feeling like I barely made it out alive, and there was no way I could survive that again with my marriage and family intact. The next fear I wrote on the paper was *being vulnerable*.

Whenever I think of vulnerability, I think about horses. When it comes to my own vulnerability, I have many negative associations—the words *weak, incompetent* and even *dangerous*. Even though horses live in a state of vulnerability every day, those same words just do not apply. With horses, words such as *strength, power* and *beauty* are much more appropriate. How do horses so gracefully deal with their vulnerability? I believe the answer is that they live in the moment.

My next homework assignment was to create a timeline from birth to present and list those events that had had an impact on me. Using a scale from one to ten, I was asked to rate how those experiences continue to affect me. That task took a little longer. There were a few events along the way that made my list up until 1996. And my timeline seemed to explode with incidents after the time I joined the RCMP—mostly scoring between four and six. There were many significant moments during that time, but they didn't preoccupy my thoughts. It was only when I spoke about them or dwelled on them that I noticed their effect.

The next sessions were spent going through each experience I had documented on my timeline. There were specific incidents, such as the one on the bridge in Prince George, but other moments (such as when I was told my career was over) still had an impact on me. I was on an emotional roller coaster—feeling anger until the tears started to flow. Then I felt anger again, because I couldn't control those emotions. After a couple of these sessions of identifying specific incidents, we felt ready to enter the next phase.

A few sessions later, my psychologist asked me if I would be surprised if she told me that I had PTSD. No, it wasn't a surprise. She asked, "How do you feel about having PTSD?" I responded, "It's just another label. It doesn't define me." And it doesn't. Let's get on to what we're going to do about it.

My lesson this time would be to learn the difference between containing these memories and finding some sort of resolution. I had successfully dealt with my experiences on a cognitive level. I understood and had worked through them in my mind. What I didn't know was that trauma lives not only in the mind, but also in every cell of my body. I was having physical and emotional reactions to events that I had cognitively filed away. This time, my body was telling my brain, *I'm not done yet.*

My psychologist asked me if I knew about Eye Movement Desensitization and Reprocessing (EMDR). I had been through one session before with a different psychologist and had had some success. The memory or experience I worked with during that session doesn't feel like it's at the forefront of my mind, but instead exists off in the distance somewhere. The point of EMDR is not to forget about experiences. The point is to stop unprocessed emotions from pouring out of one's body in various ways when one speaks about or writes about a past experience.

―――――――――

The EMDR appointments are double sessions, one hundred minutes long. My psychologist had explained EMDR completely, but I was still feeling a bit nervous when I went to my first appointment. Usually our big, comfortable chairs are facing each other, with a distance of a few feet between us. Dr. P begins arranging the furniture, so that the light bar she uses is directly in front of me as I sit in my chair. The light bar sits on a tripod with twenty-four lights spread out horizontally across the thin bar. The lights illuminate one at a time, travelling left to right and back and forth until Dr. P uses her remote control to stop them. Her chair is positioned off to my right and to the side of the light bar. She puts herself in a position to be able to observe how fast the light is travelling and if my eyes are tracking the light as it moves back and forth.

We take a moment to set the speed of the blue light travelling across the bar. Then Dr. P passes over two small pulsars that will vibrate in each of my hands in time with the light. When the light travels to the left side of the bar, my left hand will feel a vibration, and when the light passes over the middle onto the right side of the bar, the right pulsar will vibrate. There is a constant left, right, left, right pulsing, much like the practice of tapping. This sensation stops when the lights stop.

During our brief conversation before EMDR, we had discussed where in my timeline we would start. We decided to begin with the moment in the Health Services Officer's office when I was told my hearing loss was going to end my operational career.

My psychologist asks a number of questions before we begin. She asks what word best describes how I am feeling in that moment with the HSO and my immediate response is "Failure."

She starts the lights and asks me to put myself back in the office and notice how I'm feeling. I'm trying to follow the lights with my eyes, but I can also feel myself holding my breath. Her response is "Notice that," and she starts the lights again. I can feel the anxiety rising and my eyes not wanting to follow the lights. I feel a huge sense of defiance and resistance. Her response: "Notice that." I get to a point where I want to jump out of my chair. I have an overwhelmingly uncomfortable feeling. If she tells me to "notice that" one more time, we might have a problem. The anxiety is triggering my fight-or-flight response. I obviously won't attack my therapist, but I *am* ready to flee. My eyes continue to try to follow the damn blue light. And then, I feel the anxiety start to pass.

Here is how the process works: Following the lights basically gives my brain something to do so the rest of my body can get a word in edgewise. The exercise of tracking the lights painlessly preoccupies my mind, and then opens the door to body consciousness and awareness. From there the process becomes what I would call free association. Wherever my thoughts go is where I need to be. I go from experience to experience, some on my timeline and some not. Dr. P stops the lights at set time intervals, and I tell her the words and experiences that have popped into my mind. The back and forth movement of my eyes enables my brain to reprocess these memories in a different way. It is also an exercise in processing the emotions that went along with those experiences. Gone from the forefront of my mind, but not forgotten.

During my last EMDR session, I jump back and forth from being on that bridge in Prince George to being in the morgue in Brooks with the family of the teenage boy who rolled his truck. I knew I had some unresolved issues with what happened on the bridge, but the process is taking me to other places that I didn't expect to go. I'm told by Dr. P that it's common to find links between different experiences. One memory triggers another memory for a reason. It's a puzzle, and EMDR helps to put all the pieces back together.

I'm beginning to understand that it's not just the incidents themselves with which I have unfinished business. The underlying theme, at this point, appears to be moments when I have gone against myself. Times when I should have or wanted to speak, act or feel, but didn't or couldn't. Those times when I acted in a counterintuitive way. The times when my thoughts or actions violated my own personal truth. Wishing someone a harsher death: that violates my personal truth. Dragging by the hair a homeless person who threatened to hurt me: that violates my personal truth. Not feeling compassion for a family who lost their only son or brother in a rollover: that violates my personal truth.

The nightmares have stopped, but my journey continues. Resolving trauma is hard work. Damage has been done, but I owe it to myself and my family to see this through.

CHAPTER ELEVEN

Onward and Upward

The purpose of the War Horse Symposiums is to provide information about operational stress injuries and recognize the programs and services available to frontline service providers who struggle with these injuries. From my own experience, however, I learned that often information isn't enough to create change. We experience powerful moments, as I did on that bridge, moments that create shifts in our perceptions. What is required is an equally powerful *experience* to create a shift back the other way.

This change became most clear to me during the first War Horse Symposium. A new horse had just come to Riversong Ranch, and Chris was "saving" this gigantic, high-headed warmblood named Vegas specifically for this demonstration. Vegas was initially full of attitude, but Chris demonstrated—by speaking in a body language that Vegas could understand and appreciate—that the horse was actually soft and sweet and gentle.

Unexpectedly, Chris called me into the round pen and asked me to lead the horse around the pen without a rope or halter.

Vegas was free to follow me or ignore me—it all hinged on my ability to speak his language and give him enough of what he needed to feel comfortable. I was already nervous, and having Chris put me on the spot during his demonstration turned up the pressure in a big way. I had worked with a few horses previously at Riversong, but most of my experience was with Maggie. She's a smaller horse. Vegas is big and powerful.

I took a breath and said hello. I pointed to Vegas's hip and drew away with the core of my body. He looked at me as if pondering his options. Again, I put my energy on his hip to turn him in and then moved out of the way of his head, inviting him to come with me. He lowered his head and came in right behind me. We moved around that pen together, and when we came to a halt, his head was below my waist (a measure of how relaxed he was), and I looked into those big, soft brown eyes of his.

That's why I wanted to bring these people here. I wanted each of them to experience a moment just like this, because there truly is nothing like it. I wasn't nervous anymore. Just seeing the transformation in Vegas created a space in everyone there to allow that shift in perspective.

The agenda for the next morning began with another horse demonstration and the opportunity for people to participate in exercises with the horses. Chris had his horse, Dollar, brought into the arena. Dollar has a large scar on the front of his face— a souvenir from a previous owner who had hit him repeatedly with a two-by-four. Dollar would have been sent to slaughter for being "unmanageable" had Chris not purchased him—for a dollar. Here was a case of If you don't do it my way, you will suffer the consequences (a board to the head). And if you still don't do what I say, then you will be tossed aside and replaced. Everyone there could easily relate to Dollar's story.

Two people volunteered to work with Dollar. One woman was employed by Alberta Health Services and the other was a former police officer. They each took a position at Dollar's shoulder, each holding a lead rope attached to his halter. The object of the exercise was to keep Dollar pointed straight ahead and to make him feel safe and relaxed. The first thing Dollar did was back up—his non-aggressive way of saying, *With all due respect, I really don't feel comfortable being in the middle of you two.*

They had to adjust their body language and their energy in order for Dollar finally to exhale and stand still. The exercise involved blocking Dollar's head from turning into one person, and straightening him to keep him from bending his barrel into the other person. The two volunteers had to work together and stay away from Dollar's head. Everyone initially wants to go to the head of a horse, unaware that the animal feels most vulnerable when a predator (a human) goes there. For the human, the trick lies in doing not what we want to do, but what the horse needs, thereby earning the horse's trust and respect.

This simple exercise turned out to be a profound experience for one woman who participated. She would transfer what she had learned with Dollar into real life; she realized the importance of boundaries, that it's okay to say no and that she will be respected if she does say no. And that people (and horses) will test those boundaries, and it is up to her to put up a respectful block. One hour with Dollar changed how this woman lived her life.

I spoke with her several times after the symposium to support her through the courageous changes she was determined to make. I knew how she was feeling and what she was going through—because of my own experiences with horses. They just have this way of being mirrors for whoever is with them at the time. They have the ability to show you who you are, if you are willing to open your eyes and see. Time with horses can change your life—I know, because it changed mine.

——————

Horses don't care what you do for a living and they do not judge. And with very little training, someone with no experience of horses can learn to "speak" horse, a language that all horses—domestic or wild, miniature to draft—understand.

This "broken and bitter cop," as I once described myself, has been hugely helped by my connection to my own horse and to horses in general. I understood right away a salient truth: if this process helped me, it can help others. Given the number of first responders in need of assistance, and given that their stories have not been told nor their plight fully grasped, I see how important it is that the message of this book—a message of hope—be widely conveyed. In the end, this is a book about compassion, and the world could use a little more of that.

——————

One of my favourite moments from the symposiums came at the end of the one held in 2011. After lunch, the plan was that the group would be led through some work with the horses. Those who were keen to see themselves through the eyes and perspective of the horse stayed, and one of those people was a trauma psychologist, the aforementioned Dr. Jacqui Linder. She is a wonderful woman and was working on her fourth degree at the time—specializing in neuropsychology. She assists first responders, but she is also very involved in helping gang members, sex-trade workers and other high-risk groups such as victims of human trafficking.

We were sitting around debriefing after being with the horses, and we were talking about communication. I saw a tear roll down her cheek, and I asked her what had made her emotional. She said, "Can it really be that simple? That all we have to do is say what we mean and do what we say?"

She went on to say she knows that as soon as she doesn't show the emotion, when she is unable to cry, she needs to stop what she's doing. Her work will mean nothing if she no longer has the ability to show and feel compassion. This highly intellectual woman found strength and purpose in her tears, where most find weakness and shame. Talk about a whole new perspective.

———

The fourth annual symposium in 2013 was the first event I organized as a retired member of the RCMP. Many times throughout this book, I've commented on how I expected to be treated. I expected to be shunned by my peers after I took a leave of absence, I expected to be given a punishment posting after I returned to Alberta, and I expected to be treated poorly after returning to work injured physically and mentally. It occurs to me that I had some pretty low expectations. I expected to struggle to find my new identity, now that my opening line when talking with someone wasn't that I was a member of the RCMP. But horses have a way of dissolving the need for identity. Ranks and positions outside the realm of this sacred space are irrelevant. Year after year these groups of people come together to unite in the common goal of learning, experiencing and creating positive change. If I had any doubts, they were erased as soon as I arrived at Riversong Ranch.

I look forward to the symposium every year, but I was especially anticipating reuniting with Jeff. He was scheduled to put on a one-day resiliency workshop for the participants. His workshops are informative and interactive. Jeff had participated in previous symposiums, but this was the first year I had elected to do an entire day with just one presenter.

Jeff, in my opinion, is the ideal go-to guy on the clinical front. When he addresses an audience, he makes eye contact with everyone in the room. He's warm, smart and capable, and he always sprinkles his talks with stories from his own time as a cop, including those where the butt of the joke is Jeff Morley. This year he told us about how one night his wife awoke and heard what she thought were burglars outside. Jeff had just come home and he was still in uniform.

"Call 911!" his wife told him.

"I *am* 911," he replied.

Jeff has addressed audiences all across the country on trauma issues in policing—including the Canadian Association of Chiefs of Police. He has also conducted countless training sessions on conflict resolution, resilience and strategies to develop psychologically healthy workplaces. Since 2004, he's been an adjunct professor in the Department of Counselling Psychology at the University of British Columbia. And in 2012, Jeff was awarded the Queen's Diamond Jubilee Medal for his work in the area of trauma and resilience in policing.

Jeff's interactive style of presenting was perfect for the symposium's intimate gathering of thirty people. He has the ability to combine pertinent scientific or medical information with experience—whether it's his experience or that of someone else in the group. He asks questions and starts a discussion. He opens the door to himself, which allows others to feel a sense of comfort and safety. Safety from judgment. Jeff has a way of making people feel "normal," and he underscores what we have already learned about the horses—that there is strength and resilience in vulnerability.

My strategy is to start the first day off with the horses as opposed to just having the group sit and listen. It's proven to be an effective way of getting everyone to see and experience everything else from a different place mentally. The theme of that year's symposium was Putting Tools in the Toolbox. I talked about some of the ways to deal with stress—from journalling to peer support, from reiki to equine-assisted programs to meditation and exercise. The second day was filled with presentations delivered by people from a variety of organizations.

Most of those attending the symposium in 2013 would have had a notion of how horses fit into the equation, but some were no doubt still asking, What do horses have to do with operational stress injuries?

Some individuals at the symposium have horses of their own, and they were actually at a disadvantage because they would now have to unlearn habits—such as directing a horse by focusing on the horse's head. "You herd the body, you do not capture the face" is how Chris puts it.

In equine body language, even those who had never been close to a horse before would learn that everything we do with our bodies provokes a response in the horse. The angle of the hip, whether shoulders are level or not, a step back or forward: all convey precise meaning to the animal. And horses respond to that, and we then respond to their response, so what seems simple can get complicated. It's like learning any new language: hard, especially in the beginning, but delightfully rewarding when you discover that the lessons have paid off.

There was a grey named Budweiser in the paddock closest to the meeting room where the symposium took place. Chris needed Budweiser to offer some simple pointers, and he needed a volunteer. Rob—an EMT who had been off on stress-leave for almost four months—bravely put up his hand and walked into the paddock with a rope and halter in hand. He has horses at his place but they're for his wife to ride, not him. Still, he knew about going up to a horse and putting on a halter. Asked to do just that, he approached Budweiser, who was, of course, quite willing to be "caught."

With Chris both advising Rob on what to do with his body and explaining what the horse was thinking based on its body language, we could all see that the horse was reacting to very subtle changes in Rob's body language. Just changing the angle of his hip suddenly made Budweiser relax.

"Horses," Chris said, "don't respect wimps and they don't trust bullies." So if Budweiser tried to enter Ron's space with his head, Chris's instruction was to put up the closest hand as a block—not to touch the horse's head but to protect Ron's space. Horse rules. And the second that Budweiser saw Rob take charge, not in any mean way but in a clear, consistent way, he began to make licking and chewing motions with his mouth—signs of contentment.

There were many such "aha" moments that day. We had everyone working in teams, with groups of two acting as horses (imagine two people, with the one behind resting her hands on the shoulders of the one ahead) and one as horse handler. The idea was for them to practise equine language before working on actual horses. Core out, core in. Shoulders level, or tipped. The angle of the hip. Position of the hand. These all mean something specific to a horse. Humans are vertical and horses are horizontal, but we can communicate with each other as long as we understand what meaning our bodies convey to a horse and what the horse is saying in return. It was all a warm-up for the horse clinic the next day.

I had some concerns about how the second presentation would be received. I asked my good friend Sandra to come for the day and talk about the work she does. Sandra by trade is a school teacher, but she also endeavours to be a teacher of a different kind. Sandra is a highly skilled and intuitive energy practitioner.

I met Sandra when my oldest daughter started playschool about eight years ago. Sandra's oldest daughter attended the same school, and we had both just had our second daughters. We often ran into each other with sleeping infants nestled inside car seats or hanging off our arms. At the time, I was in the midst of dealing with my depression and what was left of my career. To

be honest, a friendship with a "civilian" was not what I was looking for. And yet, when she asked me to go for coffee, I said yes. It
turned out to be the beginning of a long and meaningful friendship. Sandra slowly opened my eyes to a whole new perspective,
one that was instrumental in bringing me to a place where the
world began to make sense again. She has been not only a friend
but also one of a few guides along my way.

It's hard to describe what it feels like when you get to a place
where you feel completely numb. You can't even wrap your head
around the concept of joy or happiness, let alone remember the
experience of it. There is no wonder, no anticipation, no expectation that one moment will be any better than the next; in fact,
you believe, it'll probably be worse. In such circumstances, one is
completely disconnected from everyone and everything.

The concept of energy was new to me at the time, but I was
willing to listen. Then Sandra took my hand one afternoon and
grabbed what she called a thread of energy in my palm, and I
actually *felt* it. I was hooked. After she let my hand go, I just sat
there and stared down at it, because it felt like it was on fire. And
much as with the horses, I experienced something I knew needed
to be shared with others.

The symposium was Sandra's first public showing of this
other work she does. Although she wholeheartedly believes in
it, she knows that not everyone is open to the concept of energy
healing. There were a lot of skeptics in the room, and I could feel
her nervousness as she began to speak. Shortly into her presentation she stopped for a moment. I wasn't sure if she was going to
continue. But then she took a breath and proceeded to deliver
her story in a genuine and authentic way. She ended by offering

to donate her time for the rest of the day to give participants the opportunity to experience what she does. That morning we had turned my trailer into her private working space, complete with massage table. Sandra uses a massage table, but she doesn't touch the person at all during the treatment.

I was confident that at least a few participants would take her up on her offer, but we were both amazed at the steady stream that entered the trailer. She worked through lunch and all that day.

But healing is a complicated business. Many of these first responders told stories—around the campfire, during exchanges as part of the symposium, or in private conversation—of the most harrowing kind, stories that helped explain why they were seeking respite through this symposium.

Rob, an emergency medical technician, described the events that had compelled him to take time off work. After four months away, he still could not think about going back. When there's been an accident or a heart attack, Rob and his partner show up at your door. The bright red light is flashing, the loud siren has just ceased. Help has arrived. For twenty years, this has been Rob's work. And no doubt he does it well. During a coffee break at the symposium, he came to speak to me. He wanted to talk about the circumstances that had brought him here. I had the sense that he had told his story many times before—maybe to a psychiatrist or counsellor. Maybe to a friend or relative. For the most part, he did not choke up as he spoke, but neither was he dispassionate.

In the space of four months on the job, Rob had been called to four different scenes where young people had died. He described how a four-year-old boy had slid into a river and drowned. He described fishing around in the water and finding the boy's limp body, taking him in his arms and sprinting across a field to the ambulance. "I would have died for that kid," Rob told me. They took that boy to the hospital, working on him along the way and desperately trying to revive him. At the hospital, Rob was crying, the nurses were crying, the doctor was crying.

In another case, Rob was called to the scene of a horrific accident. A grandmother had run over and killed her own grandson in a driveway. "I know of EMT people," Rob told me, "who have done the training, they see their first really bad case, and they quit on the spot." In others, he had seen the aftermath of a suicide by leatherwork knife, heads blown off by a shotgun blast, individuals with much of their torsos gone. Rob has been able to endure all that gore, but those four deaths of young people were too much for him to bear.

We are still learning about PTSD, but this much we know for certain: everyone has a breaking point.

Everyone at the symposium had stories to tell, stories of trauma inflicted, but as some of the psychologists here had told us, when the stories involve terrible things happening to children, the impact on first responders is likewise terrible.

———

During the third day, we paused in our deliberations to look out the window just as the shadows were lengthening in the pastures outside. We were gathered in a meeting room attached to the west end of the arena, and a great expanse of glass afforded a striking view to the west—of the paddocks and the fields beyond them. A hush fell over all of us as a three-point buck and several does and fawns ambled past. Horses here sometimes vacate their windbreak shelters so a newborn fawn can doze there in the sun. The deer are simply part of the cast of characters here, some feral and some domestic. Cougars, bears, elk, wolves, coyotes— all wander through at times.

A small crew of us went off to a far paddock to retrieve six horses. They were parked in stalls briefly, then let loose in the cavernous arena where they charged around, some bucking and kicking. They are all pasture-mates but now, introduced into this much smaller space, the pecking order would have to be re-established. I put everyone's name in a hat so teams could be formed, and then by the same random format were teams assigned particular horses.

Would it be little Pepsi, the smallest and most junior horse? Or Tsunami, a 17.2-hand horse (huge, in other words), or Avalon, the dominant mare in the herd? Or would it be one of two other black horses—Bahama, a still gorgeous twenty-one-year-old Shire-Thoroughbred cross or the by-now-familiar Razzy?

Part of what makes this exercise so interesting, so involving, is that someone suffering from depression cannot dwell on that fact while handling a horse. You must be there, in the moment. If you lose focus, even for an instant, you could send the wrong message or perhaps a mixed message to the horse. A handful of us—Chris, Kathryn, Shelley and I—made our rounds from team to team, offering a play-by-play and helpful instruction: *This is what you are doing right (or wrong). This is what the horse is saying in response.*

The goal was to make the horse understand, *I am surrounded by non-threatening power.* If you can create well-being and still-ness in your body, the horses will become still in their bodies. The horses will feel peace, and they will associate that peace with you.

Imagine how good that must feel. Someone traumatized by her work and long prone to depression and anger and much else, and incapable of offering comfort to anyone else, finds herself working with a horse who takes comfort in her company. The horse will test you every step of the way, for they are hard-wired as prey animals to do that: *Who is this human? Can I trust her? Does she understand me—every time? Does she cause me anguish or does she bring me peace? Can she be counted on as a worthy leader or can I dominate her?*

It feels so good when you pass those tests. The feedback is immediate. The horse's head comes up (worry) or goes down (calm). The horse twirls his tail (annoyance) or tips one hind foot while standing (a semi-snooze pose). It's profoundly simple. And simply profound.

———

The fifth annual War Horse Symposium was a significant mile-stone, and I wanted to make it memorable.

I had completed my meditation certification training in June, through Samadhi Meditation in Edmonton, and was continu-ing to discover more and more traditional and non-traditional treatment modalities. A woman from an organization called BodyTalk was interested in attending the symposium. She and her colleague offered to donate their time for the day and provide free sessions to anyone interested in learning more and experien-cing that type of energy work. Once again, my trailer was transformed into a private space. And once again, participants lined up to get a taste of what BodyTalk had to offer.

Other presenters, including Ron Campbell, offered their experience and expertise about peer support and related services and programs. Tamara Gaboury, who had attended the symposium in 2013, came back as a presenter and as the new vice-president of the War Horse Awareness Foundation. Tamara's passion for horses and first responders had been so obvious the first time we met that I asked her to be on the board of directors. The day ended with a presentation by War Horse alumna Dr. Jacqui Linder. You really do have to experience her to truly appreciate how knowledgeable and genuine she is.

As she walked back and forth across the floor with her bare feet (to ground herself), she spoke, posed questions and challenged us to challenge ourselves. She shared an intimate and personal story about her own childhood experiences, and then asked, "Do you think less of me now after I've told you my story?" Of course, everyone responded with no or a shake of their head. It was an effective way to illustrate the power in sharing one's story as opposed to the shame we are conditioned to believe we will feel instead.

I had invited Julie Salverson, a Canadian author and playwright who teaches drama and cultural studies at Queen's University in Kingston, Ontario. Julie is also a horse owner, and she had come to the 2013 symposium both as a horse woman and as a writer drawn to individuals and communities that have experienced violence or violation. In 2014, I invited her back—this time to lead an afternoon workshop.

Hers was really an afternoon spent on resilience training, but had you been at her workshop, you would have heard something unexpected: laughter and giggling. Julie deploys a theatrical form called "clown." The idea is to use absurdist humour to get people in a group to reveal truths, and sometimes very uncomfortable truths. "In clown work," says Julie, "you can look at absolutely dreadful things, but you're surprised by what you see, so you can look at it in a fresh way. I think there's a humanity that can come through."

Julie started out by having us name models of cars in rapid-fire fashion, and when someone missed a beat, we laughed. But no one was judged. That was followed by a clapping exercise, and as the group coalesced and got up and physically moved, the stories came. Julie had us adopt poses and invite the group to guess what the pose meant. We were invited to tell two stories, one true and one fabricated, and the rest had to decide which was which. Julie told me that she once did this exercise with a community group and one individual offered two stories: one had him catching a fish and winning a prize, and the other had him as a lion tamer for a Barnum & Bailey circus. Everyone picked the fish story as true, but the man then opened his shirt to show the scars where a lion had raked him with its claws.

One burly police officer told Julie after the workshop, "That was *so* much fun. You had me in the first five minutes. But next time you do one of these things, don't use the word *drama*."

The final day spent with the horses allowed everyone to take all the information from the first two days and put it all together. I enjoy this methodology with the horses, because it goes beyond providing a "feel-good" experience for people. It would be easy to bring out a few horses and have everyone lead them around in the arena. It's true, just being with a horse makes you feel good. It would be enough for most, especially for anyone who hasn't felt good in a long time. And as a participant it is easy to convince yourself that you actually made a connection, because it's been so long since you felt anything at all. So what you feel, you tell yourself, must be that connection that we as human beings are hardwired to need.

But after having experienced what I did with Maggie, I know the difference. In the beginning it was great to just be around her, but I knew on a deeper level that something wasn't quite right. Looking back now, I see that the very foundation of my frustration with her was that I could feel there was no connection. I had all these great intentions, and I cared for her more than I had cared for anything in a very long time, and yet it wasn't enough. And it triggered something. Once again, I was being denied my peace.

My choices were to become angry again (and repeat that cycle) or to choose real change. But as Dr. Linder had discussed the day before, can choice and being in the space of fight-or-flight co-exist? She does not believe they can. She believes that those who are in a state of fight-or-flight do not have the luxury of choice. They are in a highly reactive state where survival is the only objective. Fortunately, I was in a place of wellness that enabled me to understand and see that I did have a choice.

The symposium ended on a Friday, and on Saturday I drove to the airport to catch a plane to Montreal. Although I felt a little drained, my excitement for the next event kept me going.

I drove to the airport and began the initial leg of my trip to Lake Placid, New York, to launch the first PEER U.S./Canada Retreat (PEER stands for Peer Empowered Equine and Resiliency). The venue was Snowslip Farm in Lake Placid. This spectacular Adirondack setting offers a backdrop of mountains, Olympic ski jumps and about 50 hectares of breathtaking fields, woodlands, ponds and streams.

After a successful demonstration in July to potential funders and participant organizations, we had planned our first retreat for September of 2014. In just six short weeks, funds were raised for sixteen $1,000 scholarships to send first responders from Canada and the United States to participate in this unique cross-border event. The retreat was fully funded, including meals and accommodations. Participants just had to find their way to Lake Placid. Initially my intention was to find twelve first responders—six from Canada and six from the United States—but the response from the first responder community was so overwhelming that we expanded it to sixteen.

It wasn't by design, but the Canadian attendees were six active or retired members of the RCMP from across the country—British Columbia, Alberta, Quebec and Ontario. The American attendees were all from New York State, including state police and military veterans. To be able to help put on this event to serve my fellow RCMP members was nothing short of a dream come true. It felt like I had come full circle.

The retreat format was different from that of the symposium. I had been the organizer of an event for the past five years, but for this program I was retreat leader, and I found myself in uncharted territory. I am a listener, not a talker. It was uncomfortable to be responsible for leading the debriefing sessions. I'm always the last one in a group to speak (if I do at all). I prefer to take it all in, internalize and figure out what it means on my own terms and in private. But I've learned that being uncomfortable is usually synonymous with finding opportunity for growth— and that it was.

Some of the first responders who came together for this retreat had not ventured out of their comfort zones in a long time and hadn't ventured out onto the road at all. Yet they found the strength and courage to break their cycles and make the trip to Lake Placid. The anxiety of the trip almost caused more than one participant to turn around and flee back to the safety of home and family. I was and still am humbled by these fellow officers.

In the end, we all had the experience of a lifetime. As one person from the retreat put it, "How is it possible to become a family of twenty people in just four days?" It was simply unforgettable.

CHAPTER TWELVE

Through the Front Door

Connection does not manifest itself out of good intentions. Connection comes from self-awareness and mindfulness. Within my marriage, if I'm getting everything I need, I will feel happy. But if Jerry is not getting what he needs, there is no real connection. Connection is achieved only when the needs of both individuals are consciously being met. It is a process of plugging back into ourselves, the horses, nature and, eventually, humanity. And it's the equivalent of opening the window and taking in a breath of fresh air after being kept indoors for decades.

Knowing what I know, it would be going against my own personal truth to provide through the symposiums only the hollow experience of petting a horse. Kathryn has instilled in me the importance of asking, "What is the horse getting out of this?" If that question is lost, then it is nothing more than people taking from the horses and using them—and where is the compassion in that? That is one of the very reasons I lost my own faith in humanity—my awareness of people taking what wasn't theirs: someone's money, property or innocence.

I noticed in reviewing the drafts of this book that I used the expression "I broke down." To become emotional—to "break down"—has such a negative connotation. In a recent conversation with Dr. Tasleem Budhwani, she commented, "I don't see you or anyone else as damaged." We need to become aware of the language we use to describe ourselves and the injuries we deal with. I've come to believe that frame of mind does contribute to frame of body. The words *damaged, broken* and *suffering* need to be eliminated from this discussion.

Judith Herman is an associate professor of psychiatry at Harvard Medical School and the author of *Trauma and Recovery*. "The ordinary response to atrocities," she writes in that book, "is to banish them from consciousness. Certain violations of the social compact are too terrible to utter aloud: this is the meaning of the word *unspeakable*. Atrocities, however, refuse to be buried. Equally as powerful as the desire to deny atrocities is the conviction that denial does not work."

Dr. Jeff Morley makes the point that many people respond to trauma by turning to religion. But the work of first responders, he says, typically shuts down that avenue. Jeff recalled a senior member who had attended seminary before joining the RCMP, but who, after many years of trauma, pronounced, "I now believe there is no God, and if there is one, fuck him!"

Dr. Linder, too, during her presentation, asked how many people have a faith. A few hands went up. Then she told those who hadn't put their hands up to go immediately to the Internet and pick one. It's true. You have to believe in something. I'm not religious in any way. According to Jeff's research, it's normal for police officers to lose their faith. It's hard to believe in God or anything that would take part in or be responsible for all the terrible things we see day after day. For people who believe in truth, honour and justice to see and experience the world at its worst—well, the word *disappointing* doesn't quite cut it. I lost faith in any sort of God and in humanity itself. And that's when the hopelessness set in.

Faith and hope are not things that reappear overnight. While at Riversong, I became interested in animal totems. I've always felt a certain comfort in animals and to learn about them in this way resonated with me. It wasn't that I believed that every time I saw an animal, it meant something, but it made me more conscious of my surroundings, and it was an opportunity to see the world in a different way. It was a way to break old habits and ways of thinking. My mind was conditioned to believe that I should be suffering, and because it didn't know anything else, it did everything it could to keep me there. But I now believe operational stress injuries are physical injuries of the brain. And when I gave all decision-making power over to the injured part of me that wasn't functioning properly, it was like jumping on a bus and letting a blind person drive. The key, for me, was to connect my mind, body and spirit, and to find a balance within my *whole* self. Horses, meditation, yoga and energy work have all given my entire being a voice.

My life is not perfect; not all of my days are good days. Thank goodness my good days far outweigh the bad days, but that took time and work. I continue to have issues with my memory and certain situations will trigger old reactions. It could be as simple as my being in the dressing room after soccer and feeling claustrophobic. I've always had issues with putting Maggie in a horse trailer, and I finally realized that being in a tight space with an unpredictable being causes me considerable anxiety. It's also counterintuitive. But most important, I've learned to not be so hard on myself. I spent years chasing the person I used to be. I expended more energy than I had, trying to be someone I could no longer be—physically, mentally and emotionally. In doing so, I was rejecting who I am now. It took me years to forgive the RCMP, but it took even longer, and it was much more difficult, to forgive myself.

For most of my life, I never thought in terms of forgiveness. Now I do, and I have horses to thank for that. By turns, I forgave the force and my former detachment commander. Early in 2014, I invited the assistant commissioner in charge of K Division to the next War Horse Symposium—and she accepted. In the end, she was unable to come, but she did send in her place two officers—a peer-support coordinator and Ron Campbell. Although Ron, Jeff and I may come across as critics of the RCMP, we are actually three of its biggest supporters. We want the RCMP as a whole to succeed because we want the members to succeed on the job and in their lives. We are eagerly awaiting the day when we can commend the efforts of this iconic organization of which we will always be a part.

Forgiving myself, as I say, was the hardest process. The lesson of horses is this: Horses forgive, as they must. Forgiveness allows them to drop their heads and relax after a human handler or rider has frightened, offended or unnerved them. They forgive, but they do not forget. My mare Maggie taught me that simple truth.

Too many first responders are convinced they have no choices. They think they're stuck, and they give up. Even when they retire, it gets no better. I was in the dark for a long, long time, but I managed to find the light. May this book plant a little seed in some hearts.

I cannot offer a twelve-step program that will cure those trying to find a way to cope. It's not a one-size-fits-all process. The War Horse Symposiums are designed to expose participants to a variety of tools and skills, but each individual has to find out for himself or herself what works. I remember once saying to my husband that "I would do anything to change the way I feel." But at the time, that just wasn't true—it was a lie I told myself. I wouldn't try the medication on the counter, I wouldn't call the psychologist's number that my doctor had written on a piece of paper, I wouldn't try anything unconventional or new. I just kept repeating the same cycle and expecting a different result—which according to Albert Einstein is the definition of insanity. And insanity is what it felt like at times.

In her presentation, Dr. Linder said that she has two doors to her office—a front door and a back door. She asked, "Which door do you think the first responders go through?" Of course in unison we all responded, "The back door." So, this is me going through the front door. I know not everyone is ready to go through the front door. Going through the front door invites judgment and therefore shame. But I finally feel ready.

I worked hard to come to a place where I could make the *choice* to take a chance. I took a chance on a psychologist, I took a chance on yoga and meditation, and I took a chance on horses. Working with horses was the first powerful experience that opened up the gateway to my viewing the world from a completely different perspective. And all of these played a part in saving my marriage, saving my relationship with my children and saving my life.

The writing was also a part of my healing process—and that process will continue for as long as I live. I wrote the first draft as Deanna Schmaltz, but I'm not her anymore. I'm Deanna Lennox now. I came out the other side. What does that mean? It means that I will still have lows in my life, but now I am aware of those lows and aware of when I need to reach out for help. Life now is about thriving, and not, as it was for so long, about surviving.

One reason I created the War Horse Awareness Foundation was to develop a forum where first responders and their families could share their stories and insights. Some who come to the forum may not be aware that what is happening in their lives is not normal and that work-induced stress and trauma may be impacting their relationships.

For one thing, first responders work odd hours and rarely nine to five. There is pressure to say yes to overtime and double shifts. Shifts don't necessarily end when they are supposed to— not when a house is on fire or you're in the middle of a high-speed car chase. And duty may call at inopportune times, such as during a child's birthday party or a romantic night out.

First responders inevitably bring work home, so while they may be physically home, their heads are elsewhere. Perhaps you've just come from a swimming accident that may have ended well, or badly, and certain images linger. Maybe work was intensely boring that day, or maybe you were forced to use your gun.

Work-induced trauma is a constant threat to first responders. These men and women have significantly higher rates of
substance abuse and domestic violence and are six times more
likely to commit suicide than the average civilian. A police officer
is eleven times more likely to commit suicide than to be killed in
the line of duty. First responders ride an emotional roller coaster,
and the consequences may include emotional numbness, hypervigilance, insomnia, cynicism, isolationism, disturbing flash-
backs and post-traumatic stress disorder.

Post-traumatic stress disorder has emotional, sensual,
psychological and physical impacts. Unless already diagnosed,
a person with PTSD usually cannot tell you, "I have PTSD." It's
not like having a cold or the flu or a broken leg. The person
may or may not remember the traumatic event. They may, in
fact, deny that they are having any problem, other than the
day-to-day stresses of the job, when, in fact, they feel inside
that they are going crazy. Another difficulty with PTSD: there
is generally a period of time that elapses between the trauma
and when the behaviours start to show. With acute PTSD, this
is a much shorter time than with chronic PTSD, in which case,
conceivably, there can be years between the trauma and the
fallout.

Listed below are behaviours and symptoms that may be
experienced. This list is not all-inclusive, and symptoms may
indicate something other than PTSD. If it is PTSD, a person will
exhibit more than one symptom from each of the three areas,
though you may not see more than one or two.

A word of caution: a few of these behaviours are normal for
first responders. It's when they go from "normal" to the extremes

that they become abnormal. If you know the person, you know what's normal. Watch out for these changes.

Intrusion: extreme nightmares, extreme paranoia, a sense of shortened future and impending doom.

Avoidance: depression, isolation (especially from loved ones), loss of interest in sex; diminished interest in previously interesting activities, sports, people; lack of motivation, constantly fatigued; loss of faith in God; sleeping too much; addictions: alcohol, drugs, sex; previously active in their work, significant shift to doing little or nothing; increased absenteeism, weak work performance, quality of work drops significantly; just plain numbing out; stops exercise and previous self-care (poor hygiene); memory loss or poor recall; disappears for periods of time from home or work.

Arousal: problems falling asleep or staying asleep; irritability; worse than usual problems with police management and/or the public; more than usual contempt/exasperation with supervision, peers, the public; increasingly cynical about everything; sudden outbursts of anger or rage, especially overkill for the situation at hand; hypervigilance (paranoia); exaggerated startle response; obsessive behaviour (what is repressed is obsessed and acted out); compulsive behaviour (shame can power compulsion, which can become addiction); overeating: noticeable weight gain; anorexia: noticeable weight loss; previously balanced in work (perhaps one of the best), but now insatiable, as if on a crusade; more violence; more hyperactive, perhaps most of the time.

Somatic issues: problems urinating; frequent headaches; chest pains; intestinal pain; diarrhea, constipation, irritable bowel syndrome, blood in stool; very frequent belching; very high use of antacids.

These symptoms are digressive, meaning over time they will probably get worse if not treated. PTSD does not go away by itself.

For more information, please visit the War Horse Awareness Foundation at www.warhorseawareness.com.

ACKNOWLEDGMENTS

Without the support of my husband, Jerry, this book would not have been possible. There were many times when I considered dropping the project entirely, but your voice of reason was constant and always kind. Thank you for challenging me and believing in me. It's been a hell of a ride, but there's no one else I would rather have riding shotgun.

Thank you to the two most talented and beautiful girls I know, Skylar and Kassidy. Don't be afraid to spread your wings and fly, and remember . . . you can do anything.

It was an honour to work with writer and editor Lawrence Scanlan. I thank you from the bottom of my heart for your passion and willingness to take on this project. You kept me grounded and worked tirelessly for almost two years.

To my literary agent, Jackie Kaiser of Westwood Creative Artists, thank you for supporting this book from the beginning. You were a tireless source of support and literary wisdom.

I am grateful to everyone at HarperCollins Canada. I couldn't have ended up in better hands. A big thank you to my editor, Jennifer Lambert. I always felt you believed in this book. Thank you for providing the guidance needed to make it a reality. Many thanks to my managing editor, Noelle Zitzer, and to freelance editor Allyson Latta, for your diligent work.

Many friends helped me through the process of writing *Damage Done*. They offered their services as amateur editors and sounding boards at a time when I wasn't able to read over the words I had written: Trudy Iwanyshyn, Anne Beales, and Lynne and Keith Edwards.

Big horsey bows to my dear friends and War Horse board members, Shelley Ricketts and Tamara Gaboury. You are inspirations, and I treasure your work and commitment to the foundation. I am eternally grateful for your efforts and dedication to a cause that I know is close to both your hearts. It's no cliché when I say I couldn't do it without you.

Thank you to Jeff Morley and Ron Campbell. You supported me from the beginning, and that support has never waned. I consider you to be friends, mentors and unwavering sources of wisdom and encouragement.

Thank you to Kathryn Kincannon-Irwin. You shared your equine expertise, your sacred space and your friendship. Joan and Gloria will ride together for years to come.

I am grateful to Chris Irwin. Thank you for sharing your knowledge about working with horses and opening the doors to Riversong Ranch for the War Horse Symposiums.

To my ladies (and men) of soccer—whether in Prince George or Edmonton and area—the soccer community has been a steady source of support, friendship and much-needed laughter. Play on.

Many thanks to my family and friends. I know you might be shocked after you read this book. Please know and understand that there was nothing you could do other than be there in the way that you were.

I would like to thank all of those who helped make the War Horse Symposiums successful. To the Alberta Union of Provincial Employees (AUPE), which has sponsored the symposium for the last few years: your sponsorship and your support are greatly appreciated. A special thank you to Randy Corbett and Dennis Malayko of the AUPE Occupational Health and Safety Committee. Careen Condrotte, Jeremy Wagner, Cyril Gowler and Donna Watts, your dedication to your work is unmatched, and I thank you for your support. You all serve as a constant reminder that there are compassionate and noble people in this world.

Last, but certainly not least, I thank all of you who have dedicated your lives to the service of others. You are brave, and you are courageous. Stand proud, stay safe and take care of yourselves and each other. You are not alone.